P9-CJY-054

1 0 1

P A S T A

R E C I P E S

A Collection of Your Favorites

PUBLICATIONS INTERNATIONAL, LTD.

Copyright © 1998 Publications International, Ltd.
All rights reserved. This publication may not be reproduced or quoted in whole or in part by any means whatsoever without written permission from:

Louis Weber, CEO
Publications International, Ltd.
7373 North Cicero Avenue
Lincolnwood, Illinois 60646

Permission is never granted for commercial purposes.

All recipes and photographs that contain specific brand names are copyrighted by those companies and/or associations, unless otherwise specified. All photographs *except* those on pages 43, 47, 49, 117, 125, 129, 159 and 165 copyright © Publications International, Ltd.

Some of the products listed in this publication may be in limited distribution.

Front cover photography by Sacco Productions, Ltd.

Pictured on the front cover: Pasta with Shrimp, Broccoli and Red Pepper *(page 160)*.
Pictured on the back cover *(from left to right)*: Minestrone *(page 10)* and Vegetable Lasagna *(page 82)*.

ISBN: 0-7853-2801-7

Library of Congress Catalog Card Number: 97-75998

Manufactured in U.S.A.

8 7 6 5 4 3 2 1

Microwave Cooking: Microwave ovens vary in wattage. Use the cooking times as guidelines and check for doneness before adding more time.

101 PASTA RECIPES

A Collection of Your Favorites

Super

SOUPS & SALADS

Tortellini Soup

½ pound mild or hot Italian sausage links,
   in casings
1 tablespoon olive oil
1 medium onion, chopped
2 cloves garlic, minced
4 cups canned beef broth
1 can (16 ounces) whole tomatoes, drained
   and chopped
1 carrot, sliced
1 teaspoon dried oregano leaves
1 teaspoon dried basil leaves
½ teaspoon salt
¼ teaspoon black pepper
1 small zucchini, halved and sliced
1 package (9 ounces) refrigerated,
   cheese-filled tortellini*
Grated Parmesan cheese

*Do not use frozen tortellini.

1. Cook sausage in medium skillet over medium heat 7 minutes or until evenly browned. Add ½ cup water. Reduce heat to low. Cover and simmer 20 minutes. Drain; allow sausage to stand at room temperature until cool enough to handle.

2. Heat oil in 5-quart Dutch oven or large saucepan over medium heat. Cook and stir onion and garlic in oil 4 minutes or until onion is soft.

3. Stir in beef broth, tomatoes, carrot, oregano, basil, salt and pepper. Bring to a boil over high heat. Reduce heat to medium-low; simmer, uncovered, 30 minutes, stirring occasionally.

4. Cut sausage into thin slices; add to Dutch oven. Simmer 10 minutes.

5. Bring soup to a boil over high heat. Add zucchini and tortellini. Reduce heat to medium-high. Gently boil 7 minutes or until pasta is just tender.

6. Ladle into bowls. Sprinkle each serving with cheese; serve immediately.   *Makes 6 servings*

Note: Tortellini continues to absorb liquid while standing. It may be necessary to add additional broth when reheating soup.

Tortellini Soup

Chicken and Homemade Noodle Soup

¾ cup all-purpose flour
2 teaspoons finely chopped fresh thyme *or*
   ½ teaspoon dried thyme, divided
¼ teaspoon salt
1 egg yolk, beaten
1 pound boneless skinless chicken thighs
5 cups chicken broth
1 medium onion, chopped
1 medium carrot, thinly sliced
¾ cup frozen peas
   Chopped fresh parsley for garnish

1. To prepare noodles, combine flour, 1 teaspoon thyme and salt in small bowl. Add egg yolk and 3 tablespoons water; mix well. Shape into a small ball, working until mixture holds together.

2. Place dough on lightly floured surface; flatten slightly. Knead dough 5 minutes or until smooth and elastic, adding more flour to prevent sticking, if necessary. Cover with plastic wrap. Let stand 15 minutes.

3. Roll out dough to ⅛-inch thickness, or thinner, on lightly floured surface with lightly floured rolling pin. (If dough is too elastic, let it rest a few minutes.) Let rolled dough stand about 30 minutes to dry slightly. Cut into ¼-inch-wide strips with sharp knife. Cut into 1½- to 2-inch-long pieces.

4. Cut chicken into ½- to ¾-inch pieces. Combine chicken and 2 cups water in medium saucepan. Bring to a boil over high heat. Reduce heat to medium-low; cover and simmer 5 minutes. Drain; rinse chicken. Set aside.

5. Combine chicken broth, onion, carrot and remaining 1 teaspoon thyme in 5-quart Dutch oven or large saucepan. Bring to a boil over high heat. Add noodles. Reduce heat to medium-low; simmer, uncovered, 8 minutes or until noodles are tender but still firm to the bite.

6. Stir in chicken and peas. Bring soup just to a boil. Sprinkle chopped parsley over each serving.
Makes 4 servings

Chicken and Stars Soup with Peas

1½ cups Stellini, Alphabets or other small
      pasta shape, uncooked
  1 tablespoon butter or margarine
  3 medium carrots, finely diced
  2 celery ribs, finely diced
  6 cups low-sodium chicken broth, skimmed
      of fat
1½ cups diced cooked chicken
  ½ cup frozen peas, thawed
      Salt

Prepare pasta according to package directions; drain and set aside.

Melt butter or margarine in medium saucepan. Add carrots and celery. Sauté vegetables over medium heat about 7 to 10 minutes or until soft. Stir in chicken broth, diced chicken, pasta and peas. Bring soup to a boil. Season with salt to taste. Serve immediately.   *Makes 6 servings*

Favorite recipe from **National Pasta Association**

Chicken and Homemade Noodle Soup

Acorn Squash 'n' Pasta Soup

8 ounces Acine di Pepe, Ditalini or Small
    Shells, uncooked
2 medium acorn squash, split, peeled,
    seeded and quartered
2 tablespoons margarine
1 large onion, chopped
1 cup grated carrots
1½ teaspoons brown sugar
¾ teaspoon ground mace or nutmeg
½ teaspoon ground ginger
½ teaspoon cinnamon
3 (13¼-ounce) cans low-sodium chicken
    broth (about 6 cups), divided

TOPPING
1 cup nonfat sour cream
1 tablespoon granulated sugar

Cook squash in 1 inch of water in covered saucepan 15 minutes or until tender. Cool. Scrape out pulp and return to saucepan. Add margarine, onion, carrots, brown sugar, mace, ginger and cinnamon. Simmer, covered, 10 minutes, stirring occasionally. Cook until vegetables are tender. Add 3 cups chicken broth.

Purée broth mixture in blender or food processor; return to saucepan. Add remaining 3 cups of chicken broth; bring to a boil. Add pasta; cook, stirring occasionally, 10 minutes or until pasta is al dente. Before serving, blend sour cream and granulated sugar in separate bowl. Place dollop on top of each bowl of soup. Serve immediately.

Makes 4 to 6 servings

Favorite recipe from **National Pasta Association**

Chicken Rotini Soup

½ pound boneless skinless chicken breasts,
    cut into ½-inch pieces
2 tablespoons butter or margarine
4 ounces fresh mushrooms, stemmed, thinly
    sliced
½ medium onion, chopped
4 cups canned chicken broth
1 teaspoon Worcestershire sauce
¼ teaspoon dried tarragon leaves
¾ cup uncooked rotini pasta
1 small zucchini, thinly sliced
    Fresh basil for garnish

1. Combine chicken and 1 cup water in medium saucepan. Bring to a boil over high heat. Reduce heat to medium-low; simmer 2 minutes. Drain; rinse chicken.

2. Melt butter in 5-quart Dutch oven or large saucepan over medium heat. Add mushrooms and onion. Cook and stir until onion is soft. Remove from heat.

3. Stir in chicken, chicken broth, Worcestershire and tarragon. Bring to a boil over high heat. Stir in uncooked pasta. Reduce heat to medium-low; simmer, uncovered, 5 minutes.

4. Add zucchini to soup; simmer, uncovered, about 5 minutes, or until pasta is tender. Ladle into bowls. Garnish, if desired.

Makes 4 servings

Chicken Rotini Soup

Hearty Pasta and Chick-Pea Chowder

6 ounces uncooked rotini pasta
2 tablespoons olive oil
¾ cup chopped onion
½ cup chopped celery
½ cup thinly sliced carrot
2 cloves garlic, minced
¼ cup all-purpose flour
1½ teaspoons Italian seasoning
⅛ teaspoon crushed red pepper
⅛ teaspoon black pepper
2 cans (13¾ ounces each) chicken broth
1 can (19 ounces) chick-peas, rinsed and drained
1 can (14½ ounces) Italian-style stewed tomatoes, undrained
6 slices uncooked bacon

1. Cook rotini according to package directions. Rinse, drain and set aside.

2. Meanwhile, heat oil in 4-quart Dutch oven or large saucepan over medium-high heat until hot. Add onion, celery, carrot and garlic. Reduce heat to medium; cook and stir 5 to 6 minutes or until vegetables are crisp-tender.

3. Remove from heat. Stir in flour, Italian seasoning, red pepper and black pepper until well blended. Gradually stir in broth. Return to heat and bring to a boil, stirring frequently. Boil, stirring constantly, 1 minute. Reduce heat to medium. Stir in cooked pasta, chick-peas and tomatoes. Cook 5 minutes or until heated through.

4. Meanwhile, place bacon between double layer of paper towels on paper plate. Microwave on HIGH (100%) 5 to 6 minutes or until bacon is crisp. Drain and crumble. Sprinkle soup with bacon. Serve immediately. *Makes 6 servings (about 7 cups)*

Minestrone

3 slices bacon, diced
½ cup chopped onion
1 large clove garlic, finely chopped
2½ cups (two 10½-ounce cans) condensed beef broth
1½ cups water
⅔ cup (6-ounce can) CONTADINA® Dalla Casa Buitoni Tomato Paste
1 teaspoon Italian herb seasoning
¼ teaspoon ground black pepper
2 cups (2 medium) sliced zucchini
1 package (10 ounces) frozen mixed vegetables
½ cup dried small macaroni
½ cup (2 ounces) grated Parmesan cheese

COOK bacon in large saucepan over medium-high heat until crispy. Add onion and garlic. Cook for 1 to 2 minutes or until onion is tender; drain. Add broth, water, tomato paste, Italian herb seasoning and pepper; stir. Bring to a boil. Reduce heat to low; cook for 10 minutes.

ADD zucchini, mixed vegetables and pasta. Bring to a boil, stirring to break up vegetables. Reduce heat to low; cook for 8 to 10 minutes or until vegetables and pasta are tender. Serve with cheese. *Makes 8 servings*

Minestrone

Ravioli Soup

8 ounces sweet Italian sausage, casing
   removed
1 clove garlic, crushed
2 (13¾-fluid ounce) cans lower sodium
   chicken broth
2 cups water
1 (9-ounce) package frozen miniature
   cheese-filled ravioli
1 (15-ounce) can garbanzo beans, drained
1 (14½-ounce) can stewed tomatoes
⅓ cup GREY POUPON® Dijon Mustard
½ teaspoon dried oregano leaves
¼ teaspoon coarsely ground black pepper
1 cup torn fresh spinach leaves
   Grated Parmesan cheese

In 4-quart heavy pot, over medium heat, brown
sausage and cook garlic until tender, stirring to
break up sausage, about 5 minutes. Pour off excess
fat; remove sausage mixture from pot and set
aside.

In same pot, over medium-high heat, bring chicken
broth and water to a boil. Add ravioli; cook for 4
to 5 minutes or until tender. Stir in beans, stewed
tomatoes, sausage mixture, mustard, oregano and
pepper; heat through. Stir in spinach and cook
until wilted, about 1 minute. Serve topped with
Parmesan cheese.   *Makes 8 servings*

Pasta Vegetable Chowder

1 cup Small Shells, Elbow Macaroni or other
   small pasta shape, uncooked
3 cups 1% milk, divided
1 (10-ounce) box frozen mixed vegetables,
   thawed and drained, *or* 1½ cups
   chopped fresh vegetables (such as
   zucchini, yellow squash, corn and peas)
½ teaspoon dried thyme
½ teaspoon paprika
1½ teaspoons cornstarch
1 (6-ounce) can clams, drained
   Salt and ground black pepper

Prepare pasta according to package directions;
drain. Rinse pasta under cold water until cool.
Drain again.

Combine 2½ cups milk, vegetables, thyme, paprika
and pasta in 2-quart saucepan. Cook over medium
heat until bubbles form around edge of milk.

In separate bowl, combine remaining ½ cup milk
and cornstarch until cornstarch dissolves. Stir the
cornstarch mixture into soup and heat to
simmering. Add clams and simmer, stirring
frequently, 3 minutes. Add salt and pepper to
taste. Serve immediately.
                          Makes 2 to 3 servings

Favorite recipe from **National Pasta Association**

Ravioli Soup

Beef and Pasta Soup

1 tablespoon vegetable oil
½ pound round steak cut into 1-inch cubes
1 medium onion, chopped
3 cloves garlic, minced
4 cups canned beef broth
1 can (10¾ ounces) tomato pureé
2 teaspoons dried Italian seasoning
2 bay leaves
1 package (9 ounces) frozen Italian green
    beans
½ cup uncooked orzo or rosamarina
    Salt
    Lemon slices and fresh oregano for garnish
    Freshly grated Parmesan cheese (optional)
    French bread (optional)

1. Heat oil in 5-quart Dutch oven over medium-high heat; add beef, onion and garlic. Cook and stir until meat is brown and onion is slightly tender.

2. Stir in beef broth, tomato pureé, Italian seasoning and bay leaves. Bring to a boil over high heat. Reduce heat to medium-low; simmer, uncovered, 45 minutes.

3. Add beans and uncooked pasta. Bring to a boil over high heat. Simmer, uncovered, 8 minutes or until beans and pasta are tender, stirring frequently. Season with salt to taste.

4. If soup becomes too thick on standing, stir in a little water and heat through. Remove bay leaves. Ladle into bowls. Garnish, if desired. Serve with freshly grated Parmesan cheese and French bread, if desired. *Makes 5 servings*

Pasta e Fagiole

1 teaspoon olive oil
3 cloves garlic, minced
1 can (15-ounces) cannellini or Great
    Northern beans, rinsed and drained
2 cans (about 14 ounces each) fat-free
    reduced-sodium chicken broth
½ cup white wine, divided
1 tablespoon dried basil leaves
½ teaspoon black pepper
¼ to ½ teaspoon red pepper flakes
6 ounces uncooked ditalini pasta or other
    small tube pasta
4 teaspoons grated Parmesan cheese
    Fresh basil leaves for garnish

1. Heat oil in large saucepan over medium-low heat until hot. Add garlic and beans; cook and stir 3 minutes. Add chicken broth, ¼ cup wine, basil, black pepper and red pepper flakes. Bring to a boil over medium-high heat.

2. Add pasta; cook 10 to 12 minutes or until tender. Add remaining ¼ cup wine just prior to pasta being fully cooked. Sprinkle with grated cheese. Serve immediately. Garnish with fresh basil leaves, if desired.

Makes 4 (1-cup) servings

Note: This soup will be very thick.

Beef and Pasta Soup

Creamy Shell Soup

3 to 4 bone-in chicken pieces
1 cup diced yellow onions
¼ cup chopped celery
¼ cup minced fresh parsley *or* 1 tablespoon
    dried parsley flakes
1 bay leaf
1 teaspoon salt
¼ teaspoon ground white pepper
2 medium potatoes, diced
4 to 5 green onions, chopped
3 chicken bouillon cubes
½ teaspoon seasoned salt
½ teaspoon poultry seasoning
4 cups milk
2 cups medium shell macaroni, cooked and
    drained
¼ cup butter or margarine
¼ cup all-purpose flour
    Salt and ground black pepper
    Ground nutmeg and chopped fresh parsley
    for garnish

Bring 4 cups water, chicken, diced onions, celery, minced parsley, bay leaf, salt and pepper to a boil in Dutch oven. Simmer over medium heat until chicken is tender. Remove bay leaf; discard. Remove chicken; cool. Remove skin and bones from chicken. Cut chicken into small cubes; set aside.

Add potatoes, green onions, bouillon cubes, seasoned salt and poultry seasoning to broth. Simmer 15 minutes. Add milk, macaroni and chicken; return to simmer. Melt butter in small skillet over medium heat. Add flour, stirring

constantly, until mixture begins to brown. Add to soup; blend well. Simmer over low heat 20 minutes. Season to taste with salt and pepper. Garnish, if desired. *Makes 8 servings*

Favorite recipe from **North Dakota Wheat Commission**

Hearty Minestrone Soup

2 cans (10¾ ounces each) condensed Italian
    tomato soup
3 cups water
3 cups cooked vegetables, such as zucchini,
    peas, corn or beans
2 cups cooked ditalini pasta
1⅓ cups (2.8-ounce can) FRENCH'S® French
    Fried Onions

Combine soup and water in large saucepan. Add vegetables and pasta. Bring to a boil. Reduce heat. Cook until heated through, stirring often.

Place French Fried Onions on microwavable dish. Microwave on HIGH (100%) 1 minute or until onions are golden.

Ladle soup into individual bowls. Sprinkle with French Fried Onions. *Makes 6 servings*

Prep Time: 10 minutes
Cook Time: 5 minutes

Creamy Shell Soup

Sicilian-Style Pasta Salad

8 ounces dried rotini pasta, cooked, drained and chilled
1¾ cups (14-ounce can) CONTADINA®
   Dalla Casa Buitoni Pasta Ready
   Chunky Tomatoes Primavera, undrained
6 ounces cooked medium shrimp
1 cup (3.8-ounce can) sliced ripe olives, drained
¼ cup (1 ounce) grated Parmesan cheese
3 tablespoons red wine vinegar
¼ teaspoon salt

COMBINE pasta, tomatoes and juice, shrimp, olives, cheese, vinegar and salt in medium bowl; toss well. Cover; chill for at least 1 hour.

Note: For a more colorful salad, add sliced zucchini and bell peppers.

Makes 6 to 8 servings

Zesty Pasta Salad

3 cups uncooked rotini pasta
1 cup olive oil vinaigrette salad dressing
¼ cup FRENCH'S® Deli Brown Mustard
¼ cup chopped fresh basil *or* 2 teaspoons dried basil leaves
1⅓ cups (2.8-ounce can) FRENCH'S® French Fried Onions, divided
2 cups cut-up fresh vegetables, such as broccoli, carrots, zucchini or sugar snap peas

Cook pasta according to package directions using shortest cooking time. Drain and rinse.

Combine salad dressing, mustard and basil in small bowl; mix well. Combine pasta, ⅔ cup French Fried Onions and vegetables in large bowl. Pour dressing mixture over salad; toss well to coat evenly. Cover; refrigerate until ready to serve. Sprinkle with remaining ⅔ cup onions just before serving.

Makes 8 servings

Mediterranean Pasta Salad

1 package (8 ounces) refrigerated or frozen cheese tortellini
1 package (9 ounces) DOLE® Italian Style Vegetables
1 can (8 ounces) DOLE® Pineapple Chunks
2 tablespoons balsamic or red wine vinegar
1 tablespoon olive or vegetable oil
¼ pound fresh link turkey sausage, cooked, drained and sliced
1 medium DOLE® Red, Yellow or Green Bell Pepper, cut into 1-inch pieces

• **Prepare** tortellini as package directs, except add Italian style vegetables during last 2 minutes of cooking; reserve seasoning packet. Drain.

• **Drain** pineapple; reserve ¼ cup juice. Combine reserved juice, vinegar, oil and seasoning packet in large serving bowl.

• **Add** tortellini, vegetables, sausage, bell pepper and pineapple to dressing; toss to evenly coat. Serve at room temperature or chilled. Toss before serving. Garnish with fresh herbs, if desired.

Makes 6 servings

Sicilian-Style Pasta Salad

Oriental Steak Salad

1 package (3 ounces) Oriental flavor instant
    ramen noodles
4 cups water
1 bag (16 ounces) BIRDS EYE® frozen
    Farm Fresh Mixtures Cauliflower,
    Carrots & Snow Pea Pods
2 tablespoons vegetable oil
1 pound boneless beef top loin steak, cut
    into thin strips
⅓ cup Oriental sesame salad dressing
¼ cup chow mein noodles
    Lettuce leaves

• Reserve seasoning packet from noodles.

• In large saucepan, bring water to boil. Add
ramen noodles and vegetables; return to boil and
cook 3 minutes, stirring occasionally. Drain.

• Meanwhile, heat oil in large nonstick skillet
over medium-high heat. Add beef; cook and stir
about 8 minutes or until browned.

• Stir in reserved seasoning packet until beef is
well coated.

• In large bowl, toss together beef, vegetables,
ramen noodles and salad dressing. Sprinkle with
chow mein noodles. Serve over lettuce.

Makes 4 servings

Prep Time: 10 minutes

Cook Time: 11 to 12 minutes

Serving Suggestion: Salad also can be served
chilled. Moisten with additional salad dressing, if
necessary. Sprinkle with chow mein noodles and
spoon over lettuce just before serving.

Tortellini Asparagus Toss

1 pound fresh asparagus, cut into ½-inch
    pieces
2 cups tightly packed fresh spinach leaves
1 cup diced red bell pepper
2 packages (9 ounces each) small cheese-
    filled tortellini, cooked, drained and
    cooled
¼ cup red wine vinegar
2 tablespoons olive oil
1½ teaspoons lemon juice
1 teaspoon sugar
1 teaspoon LAWRY'S® Garlic Salt

Place asparagus on steamer rack; place in deep
pot with 1-inch boiling water. Cover and steam
10 minutes. Remove and set aside. Steam spinach
on steamer rack in same pot about 45 seconds or
until just wilted.

In large bowl, combine asparagus, spinach, red
pepper and tortellini; blend well. In small bowl,
combine vinegar, oil, lemon juice, sugar and
Garlic Salt; blend well. Pour over tortellini
mixture; toss well.   *Makes 4 servings*

Hints: 1½ cups broccoli flowerettes can be
substituted for asparagus. Chopped pimientos can
be substituted for red bell pepper.

Oriental Steak Salad

Garden Vegetable Pasta Salad with Bacon

12 ounces uncooked rotini or spiral pasta
½ pound bacon, thinly sliced
1 medium bunch broccoli, cut into florets
2 medium carrots, sliced diagonally
2 ribs celery, sliced diagonally
1 can (14½ ounces) pasta-ready tomatoes, drained
10 medium mushrooms, thinly sliced
½ medium red or yellow onion, thinly sliced
1 bottle (8 ounces) ranch salad dressing
½ cup (2 ounces) shredded Cheddar cheese
1 tablespoon dried parsley flakes
2 teaspoons dried basil leaves
¼ teaspoon black pepper

1. Cook pasta according to package directions. Drain and rinse well under cold water until pasta is cool.

2. Cook bacon in large skillet over medium-high heat until browned. Remove bacon from skillet; drain on paper towels. Cool and crumble into small pieces.

3. Combine broccoli, carrots, celery, tomatoes, mushrooms and onion in large bowl. Add pasta and bacon; toss lightly. Add salad dressing, Cheddar cheese, parsley, basil and pepper; stir to combine.   *Makes 6 servings*

Pea Salad with Pasta and Cheese

2 cups uncooked macaroni
1 box (10 ounces) BIRDS EYE® frozen Green Peas
6 ounces Monterey Jack, Swiss or Cheddar cheese (or any combination), cubed
½ cup light mayonnaise
¼ cup sliced green onions

• In large saucepan, cook pasta according to package directions. Add peas during last 7 minutes; drain and refrigerate until chilled.

• In large bowl, toss together pasta, peas, cheese, mayonnaise and onions until blended.
Makes 4 servings

Prep Time: 5 minutes

Cook Time: 12 to 15 minutes

Variation: Stir in ½ teaspoon celery salt for added flavor.

Garden Vegetable Pasta Salad with Bacon

Peppercorn Pasta and Bean Salad

8 ounces uncooked rotelle or radiatore pasta
1 bag (16 ounces) BIRDS EYE® frozen Farm Fresh Mixtures Broccoli, Red Peppers, Onions & Mushrooms
1 can (15 ounces) garbanzo beans (chick-peas), drained
½ cup creamy peppercorn ranch salad dressing

• In large saucepan, cook pasta according to package directions. Add vegetables during last 7 minutes; drain in colander. Rinse under cold water to cool.

• In large bowl, combine pasta, vegetables, beans and dressing. Cover and refrigerate until ready to serve.   *Makes 4 servings*

Prep Time: 5 minutes

Cook Time: 10 to 12 minutes

Variation: Add 1 can (6 ounces) tuna or salmon, drained and flaked, or 6 ounces cooked shrimp or cubed cooked chicken to the pasta mixture.

Italian Pasta & Vegetable Salad

8 ounces uncooked rotelle or spiral pasta
2½ cups assorted cut-up fresh vegetables (broccoli, carrots, tomatoes, bell peppers, cauliflower, onions and mushrooms)
½ cup cubed cheddar or mozzarella cheese
⅓ cup sliced pitted ripe olives (optional)
1 cup WISH-BONE® Italian Dressing

Cook pasta according to package directions; drain and rinse with cold water until completely cool.

In large bowl, combine all ingredients except Italian dressing. Add dressing; toss well. Serve chilled or at room temperature.
   Makes 8 side-dish servings

Note: If preparing a day ahead, refrigerate, then stir in ¼ cup additional Wish-Bone Dressing before serving.

Also terrific with WISH-BONE® Robusto Italian, Fat Free Italian, Classic House Italian, Creamy Roasted Garlic, Fat Free Creamy Roasted Garlic, Ranch, Lite Ranch, Fat Free Ranch, Creamy Caesar, Parmesan & Onion, Fat Free Parmesan & Onion, Red Wine Vinaigrette or Fat Free Red Wine Vinaigrette Dressing.

Peppercorn Pasta and Bean Salad

Tangy Garlic Tortellini Salad

¼ cup mayonnaise
¼ cup plain yogurt
1 tablespoon plus 1½ teaspoons lemon juice
1 tablespoon olive oil
2 teaspoons chopped fresh chives *or* ¼ cup
    chopped green onions
1 teaspoon LAWRY'S® Seasoned Pepper
1 to 1¼ teaspoons LAWRY'S® Garlic Salt
9 ounces fresh cheese-filled tortellini *or*
    8 ounces spiral pasta, cooked and
    drained
1 red bell pepper, cut into ¼ inch pieces
1 zucchini, cut into julienne strips
2 carrots, cut into julienne strips

In small bowl, combine all ingredients except pasta and vegetables; mix well. In medium bowl, combine pasta and vegetables; mix lightly. Add dressing; toss lightly to coat. Refrigerate at least 30 minutes.   *Makes 4 to 6 servings*

Presentation: Serve with crusty French or sourdough bread.

Grilled Pasta Salad

4 medium zucchini and/or yellow squash,
    sliced
1 medium Spanish onion, halved and cut
    into large chunks
1 envelope LIPTON® Recipe Secrets Savory
    Herb with Garlic Soup Mix*
¼ cup olive or vegetable oil
8 ounces penne, rotini or ziti pasta, cooked
    and drained
¾ cup diced roasted red peppers
¼ cup red wine vinegar, apple cider vinegar
    or white wine vinegar

*Also terrific with LIPTON® Recipe Secrets Golden Onion Soup Mix.

On heavy-duty aluminum foil or broiler pan, arrange zucchini and onion. Blend savory herb with garlic soup mix and oil. Brush over vegetables. Grill or broil 5 minutes or until golden brown and crisp-tender.

In large bowl, toss cooked pasta, vegetables, roasted peppers and vinegar. Serve warm or at room temperature.   *Makes about 4 main-dish
or 8 side-dish servings*

Tangy Garlic Tortellini Salad

Baja-Style Chili Pepper Penne Salad

1 (12-ounce) package PASTA LABELLA®
    Chili Pepper Penne Rigate
¾ cup julienned carrots
¾ cup julienned red onion
¾ cup diced seeded peeled cucumber
¾ cup chopped avocado
¼ cup chopped cilantro
⅓ cup extra-virgin olive oil
¼ cup white wine vinegar
¼ cup fresh lime juice
1 teaspoon dried oregano leaves
½ teaspoon onion powder
½ teaspoon garlic powder
    Salt and pepper, to taste
⅓ cup grated Romano cheese

Cook pasta according to package directions. When pasta is al dente, drain and rinse with cold water until cool to touch. Transfer to large mixing bowl. Add carrots, onion, cucumber, avocado and cilantro to pasta.

In small mixing bowl, whisk together olive oil, vinegar, lime juice and all remaining spices. Pour dressing over pasta mixture. Toss well. Sprinkle with Romano cheese and serve.

Makes 4 servings

Caesar Shrimp Pasta Salad

1 can (14½ ounces) DEL MONTE®
    FreshCut™ Diced Tomatoes with Garlic
    & Onion, undrained
1 pound cooked tiny shrimp
6 cups cooked corkscrew pasta or other
    small pasta
1 small cucumber, diced
1 cup Caesar dressing
3 green onions, sliced

1. Drain tomatoes, reserving ⅓ cup liquid. In large bowl, combine reserved tomato liquid with tomatoes and remaining ingredients. Season with salt and pepper to taste, if desired.

2. Cover and refrigerate until serving time. Garnish, if desired.   *Makes 4 servings*

Prep Time: 10 minutes

Caesar Shrimp Pasta Salad

Tarragon Tuna Pasta Salad

½ cup mayonnaise
½ teaspoon dried tarragon or thyme, crushed
3 cups chilled cooked mostaccioli or elbow macaroni
2 stalks celery, sliced
1 can (6½ ounces) solid white tuna in water, drained and broken into bite-sized pieces
1 can (14½ ounces) DEL MONTE® Peas and Carrots, drained

1. In large bowl, combine mayonnaise and tarragon. Add pasta, celery and tuna. Gently stir in peas and carrots.

2. Line serving plates with lettuce, if desired. Top with salad. Garnish, if desired.

Makes 4 servings

Prep Time: 8 minutes

Healthy Hint: Use light mayonnaise instead of regular mayonnaise.

French's® Favorite Macaroni Salad

8 ounces uncooked medium shell pasta
⅓ cup reduced-fat sour cream
⅓ cup reduced-fat mayonnaise
⅓ cup FRENCH'S® Deli Brown Mustard
1 tablespoon cider vinegar
3 cups bite-sized fresh vegetables, such as tomatoes, peppers, carrots and celery
¼ cup minced green onions

1. Cook pasta according to package directions using shortest cooking time; rinse with cold water and drain.

2. Combine sour cream, mayonnaise, mustard and vinegar in large bowl. Add pasta, vegetables and green onions. Toss gently to coat evenly. Season to taste with salt and pepper. Cover; chill in refrigerator 30 minutes. Stir before serving.

Makes 6 (1-cup) servings

Prep Time: 20 minutes
Chill Time: 30 minutes

Tarragon Tuna Pasta Salad

Tuscan Tuna Stuffed Pasta Salad

16 uncooked jumbo pasta shells
½ cup balsamic vinaigrette salad dressing
¼ cup chopped fresh basil or parsley
½ teaspoon salt
⅛ teaspoon black pepper
1 can (15 ounces) white kidney beans, rinsed and drained
1 can (6 ounces) white tuna packed in water, drained and flaked
1 jar (4 ounces) chopped pimiento, rinsed and drained
1⅓ cups (2.8-ounce can) FRENCH'S® French Fried Onions, divided

Cook pasta shells according to package directions using shortest cooking time. Drain; rinse under cold running water. Set aside.

Combine salad dressing, basil, salt and pepper in medium bowl; whisk until well blended. Stir in beans, tuna, pimiento and ⅔ *cup* French Fried Onions. Spoon 3 tablespoons bean mixture into each pasta shell. Sprinkle with remaining ⅔ *cup* onions.   *Makes 4 main course or 8 appetizer servings*

Prep Time: 20 minutes
Cook Time: 10 minutes

Pasta and Walnut Fruit Salad

½ of a (1-pound) package medium shell pasta, uncooked
1 (8-ounce) container nonfat plain yogurt
¼ cup frozen orange juice concentrate, thawed
1 (15-ounce) can juice-packed mandarin oranges, drained
1 cup seedless red grapes, cut into halves
1 cup seedless green grapes, cut into halves
1 apple, cored and chopped
½ cup sliced celery
½ cup walnut halves

Cook shells according to package directions; drain. Blend yogurt and orange juice concentrate in small bowl. Combine shells and remaining ingredients in large bowl. Add yogurt mixture; toss well to coat evenly. Cover; chill thoroughly.
                     Makes 6 to 8 servings

Favorite recipe from **Walnut Marketing Board**

Tuscan Tuna Stuffed Pasta Salad

Pasta Niçoise

12 ounces uncooked rotini
 1 bottle (8 ounces) Italian vinaigrette salad
    dressing, divided
 1 can (6 ounces) tuna packed in water,
    drained
 3 eggs, hard boiled, peeled and cut into
    wedges
 1 cup frozen green beans, thawed
 ¼ cup pitted black olives

1. Cook pasta according to package directions; drain.

2. Reserve ¼ cup vinaigrette. Toss pasta with remaining vinaigrette; place in serving bowl or on individual plates.

3. Arrange tuna, eggs, green beans and olives on top of pasta. Drizzle with reserved vinaigrette. Serve chilled or at room temperature.

Makes 6 servings

Roast Beef and Pasta Salad

 9 ounces uncooked radiatore pasta
 6 ounces lean roast beef
 1 can (15 ounces) kidney beans, rinsed and
    drained
 1 can (15 ounces) whole baby corn, rinsed
    and drained
 1 can (10 ounces) diced tomatoes and green
    chilies
 1 cup cherry tomato halves
 ½ cup sliced ripe olives (optional)
 2 tablespoons minced fresh parsley
 1 tablespoon minced fresh oregano
 ¼ cup olive oil
    Oregano sprigs for garnish

1. Cook pasta according to package directions; drain. Rinse in cold water; drain.

2. Slice beef into thin strips. Combine pasta, beef and remaining ingredients in large bowl. Toss to coat. Garnish with fresh oregano, if desired.

Makes 6 servings

Pasta Niçoise

Fabulous

FAMILY FAVORITES

Spaghetti Alla Bolognese

2 tablespoons olive oil
1 medium onion, chopped
1 pound ground beef
½ small carrot, finely chopped
½ rib celery, finely chopped
1 cup dry white wine
½ cup milk
⅛ teaspoon ground nutmeg
1 can (14½ ounces) whole peeled tomatoes,
　　undrained
1 cup beef broth
3 tablespoons tomato paste
1 teaspoon salt
1 teaspoon dried basil leaves
½ teaspoon dried thyme leaves
⅛ teaspoon black pepper
1 bay leaf
1 pound uncooked dry spaghetti
1 cup freshly grated Parmesan cheese
　　Fresh thyme sprig for garnish

1. Heat oil in large skillet over medium heat. Cook and stir onion until soft. Crumble beef into onion mixture. Brown 6 minutes, stirring to separate meat, or until meat just loses its pink color. Spoon off and discard fat.

2. Stir carrot and celery into meat mixture; cook 2 minutes over medium-high heat. Stir in wine; cook 4 to 6 minutes or until wine has evaporated. Stir in milk and nutmeg; reduce heat to medium and cook 3 to 4 minutes until milk has evaporated. Remove from heat.

3. Press tomatoes and juice through sieve into meat mixture; discard seeds.

4. Stir beef broth, tomato paste, salt, basil, thyme, pepper and bay leaf into tomato-meat mixture. Bring to a boil over medium-high heat; reduce heat to low. Simmer, uncovered, 1 to 1½ hours until most of liquid has evaporated and sauce thickens, stirring frequently. Remove and discard bay leaf.

5. To serve, cook spaghetti in large pot of boiling salted water 8 to 12 minutes just until *al dente*; drain well. Combine hot spaghetti and meat sauce in serving bowl; toss lightly. Sprinkle with cheese. Garnish, if desired.

Makes 4 to 6 servings

Spaghetti Alla Bolognese

Pasta, Chicken & Broccoli Pesto Toss

4 ounces (about 2 cups) vegetable spiral
   pasta, cooked and drained
2 cups cubed, cooked chicken or turkey
   breast meat
2 cups small broccoli florets, cooked until
   crisp-tender and cooled
1½ cups (6 ounces) SARGENTO® Fancy
   Supreme Shredded Low Moisture
   Part-Skim Mozzarella Cheese
⅔ cup lightly packed fresh basil leaves
2 cloves garlic
1 cup mayonnaise
1 tablespoon lemon juice
½ teaspoon salt
½ cup (2 ounces) SARGENTO® Fancy
   Supreme Shredded Parmesan Cheese
½ cup pine nuts or coarsely chopped
   walnuts, toasted

Combine pasta, chicken, broccoli and mozzarella
cheese in large bowl. Place basil and garlic in
blender or food processor container; cover. Blend
until finely chopped. Add mayonnaise, lemon
juice and salt; blend thoroughly. Stir in Parmesan
cheese. Add to pasta mixture; toss to coat. Stir
in pine nuts. Serve immediately or cover and
refrigerate. For maximum flavor, remove from
refrigerator 30 minutes before serving; toss gently.
Makes 8 servings

Fettuccine Alfredo

2 teaspoons margarine
3 cloves garlic, finely chopped
4½ teaspoons all-purpose flour
1½ cups skim milk
½ cup Parmesan cheese
3½ teaspoons Neufchâtel cheese
¼ teaspoon white pepper
4 ounces hot cooked fettuccine
¼ cup chopped fresh parsley

Melt margarine in medium saucepan over low
heat. Add garlic. Cook and stir 1 minute. Stir in
flour. Gradually stir in milk. Cook, stirring
constantly, until sauce thickens. Add cheeses and
pepper; cook until melted. Serve on fettuccine;
top with parsley. *Makes 4 servings*

Fettuccine Alfredo

Beef Stroganoff

8 ounces uncooked egg noodles
¼ cup all-purpose flour
½ teaspoon salt
¼ teaspoon black pepper
1¼ pounds beef tenderloin tips or tenderloin,
     ½ inch thick
¼ cup butter, divided
¾ cup chopped onion
12 ounces fresh button mushrooms, cleaned
     and sliced
1 can (10½ ounces) condensed beef broth
2 tablespoons tomato paste
1 tablespoon Worcestershire sauce
1 cup sour cream, at room temperature
     Fresh chives for garnish

1. Cook noodles according to package directions; drain and keep warm.

2. Meanwhile, combine flour, salt and pepper in large resealable plastic food storage bag. Cut beef into 1½×½-inch strips; add ½ of beef to flour mixture. Seal bag; shake to coat well. Repeat with remaining beef.

3. Melt 1 tablespoon butter in large nonstick skillet over medium-high heat. Add ½ of beef mixture to skillet. Cook and stir until browned on all sides. (Do not overcook.) Transfer to medium bowl. Repeat with 1 tablespoon butter and remaining beef mixture; transfer to same bowl. Set aside.

4. Melt remaining 2 tablespoons butter in same skillet over medium-high heat. Add onion; cook 5 minutes, stirring occasionally. Add mushrooms; cook and stir 5 minutes or until mushrooms are tender. Stir in broth, tomato paste and Worcestershire; bring to a boil, scraping up any browned bits.

5. Return beef mixture and any accumulated juices to skillet; cook about 5 minutes or until heated through and sauce thickens. Stir in sour cream; heat through. (Do not boil.)

6. Serve beef mixture over noodles. Garnish, if desired.   *Makes 4 servings*

Easy Fettuccine Alfredo

1 package(8 ounces) PHILADELPHIA
     BRAND® Cream Cheese, cubed
1 cup (4 ounces) KRAFT® Shredded
     Parmesan Cheese
½ cup (1 stick) butter or margarine
½ cup milk
8 ounces fettuccine, cooked, drained

STIR cream cheese, Parmesan cheese, butter and milk in large saucepan on low heat until smooth.

ADD fettuccine; toss lightly. Serve with additional Parmesan cheese, if desired.
                    Makes 4 servings

Prep Time: 5 minutes
Cook Time: 15 minutes

Beef Stroganoff

Roasted Red Pepper Pasta with Shrimp

1 jar (7 ounces) roasted red peppers packed
   in oil, undrained
2 tablespoons finely chopped fresh basil
   leaves,* divided
2 teaspoons finely chopped garlic, divided
2 tablespoons olive or vegetable oil
1 pound uncooked medium shrimp
2 tablespoons dry white wine
1½ cups water
½ cup milk
1 package LIPTON® Noodles & Sauce—
   Alfredo
   Ground black pepper to taste

*Substitution: Use 1 teaspoon dried basil leaves.

In food processor or blender, process red peppers,
1 tablespoon basil and 1 teaspoon garlic until
smooth; set aside.

In 12-inch skillet, heat oil over medium-high
heat and cook remaining 1 teaspoon garlic with
shrimp, stirring constantly, until shrimp turn
pink; remove and set aside.

In same skillet, add wine and cook 1 minute.
Add water and milk; bring to a boil. Stir in
noodles & sauce—Alfredo, then simmer, stirring
occasionally, 8 minutes or until noodles are
tender. Stir in red pepper purée and black pepper;
heat through. To serve, arrange shrimp over
noodles, then sprinkle with remaining 1
tablespoon basil. Garnish, if desired, with fresh
basil.　　　　　　　　*Makes about 4 servings*

Tuna Vegetable Medley

8 ounces cooked egg noodles
1 package (10 ounces) frozen chopped
   broccoli, thawed and well drained
1 package (10 ounces) frozen carrots,
   thawed and well drained
1 cup corn
1 can (10¾ ounces) cream of mushroom
   soup
1 can (12 ounces) STARKIST® Solid White
   or Chunk Light Tuna, drained and
   chunked
⅔ cup milk
1 cup shredded Swiss, Cheddar or Monterey
   Jack Cheese
   Salt and pepper to taste
¼ cup grated Parmesan cheese

In large bowl, combine all ingredients except
Parmesan cheese; mix well. Pour mixture into
2-quart baking dish; top with Parmesan cheese.
Bake in 400°F oven 20 to 30 minutes or until
thoroughly heated and golden on top.
　　　　　　　　　　　　Makes 6 servings

Prep Time: 40 minutes

Roasted Red Pepper Pasta with Shrimp

Hungarian Beef Goulash

¼ cup all-purpose flour
1 tablespoon Hungarian sweet paprika
1½ teaspoons salt
½ teaspoon Hungarian hot paprika
½ teaspoon black pepper
2 pounds beef stew meat (1¼-inch pieces)
4 tablespoons vegetable oil, divided
1 large onion, chopped
3 cloves garlic, minced
2 cans (about 14 ounces each) beef broth
1 can (14½ ounces) stewed tomatoes, undrained
1 tablespoon dried marjoram leaves
1 large green bell pepper, seeded and chopped
3 cups uncooked thin egg noodle twists
Sour cream

1. Combine flour, sweet paprika, salt, hot paprika and black pepper in resealable plastic food storage bag. Add ½ of beef. Seal bag; shake to coat well. Repeat with remaining beef.

2. Heat 4½ teaspoons oil in Dutch oven or large saucepan over medium heat until hot. Add ½ of beef; brown on all sides. Transfer to large bowl. Repeat with 4½ teaspoons oil and remaining beef; transfer to same bowl.

3. Heat remaining 1 tablespoon oil in same Dutch oven; add onion and garlic. Cook 8 minutes or until tender, stirring often.

4. Return beef and any juices to Dutch oven. Add broth, tomatoes with liquid, 1 cup water and marjoram. Bring to a boil over medium-high heat. Reduce heat to medium-low; cover and simmer 1½ hours or until meat is tender, stirring once.

5. Stir in bell pepper and noodles; cover. Simmer about 8 minutes or until noodles are tender, stirring once. To serve, ladle into 8 soup bowls. Dollop with sour cream.   *Makes 8 servings*

Superb Stroganoff

1 pound sirloin steak, cut into thin strips
2 tablespoons vegetable oil
½ cup chopped onion
1 can (4 ounces) mushrooms, drained
1 bag (16 ounces) BIRDS EYE® frozen Pasta Secrets Creamy Peppercorn
⅔ cup sour cream

• In large skillet, brown steak in oil over medium heat, stirring frequently.

• Stir in onion and mushrooms; cook 5 minutes or until onion is tender.

• Stir in Pasta Secrets and ¼ cup water; cover and cook over medium heat 5 minutes or until pasta is tender. Reduce heat to low; stir in sour cream. Cook until heated through.
          Makes 4 servings

Prep Time: 5 minutes
Cook Time: 20 minutes

Hungarian Beef Goulash

String Pie

1 pound ground beef
½ cup chopped onion
¼ cup chopped green bell pepper
1 jar (15½ ounces) spaghetti sauce
8 ounces spaghetti, cooked and drained
⅓ cup grated Parmesan cheese
2 eggs, beaten
2 teaspoons butter
1 cup cottage cheese
½ cup (2 ounces) shredded mozzarella cheese

Preheat oven to 350°F. Cook beef, onion and bell pepper in large skillet over medium-high heat until meat is brown, stirring to separate meat. Drain fat. Stir in spaghetti sauce; mix well.

Combine spaghetti, Parmesan cheese, eggs and butter in large bowl; mix well. Place in bottom of 13×9-inch pan. Spread cottage cheese over top. Pour sauce mixture over cottage cheese. Sprinkle mozzarella cheese over top. Bake about 20 minutes or until cheese melts.

Makes 6 to 8 servings

Favorite recipe from **North Dakota Beef Commission**

Ranch Stroganoff

1½ pounds flank steak or top sirloin steak
2 packages (1 ounce each) HIDDEN VALLEY RANCH® Milk Recipe Original Ranch® Salad Dressing mix
¼ cup all-purpose flour
¼ cup vegetable oil
¼ cup minced onion
1 clove garlic, minced
½ pound fresh mushrooms, thinly sliced
1½ cups milk
8 ounces wide egg noodles, cooked and buttered
1 tablespoon poppy seeds

Cut steak diagonally into 2×½-inch strips; set aside. Combine salad dressing mix and flour in plastic bag. Add steak and dredge with flour mixture. Place steak on platter; reserve extra coating mixture. In large skillet, heat oil over medium heat until hot. Add onion and garlic; sauté 1 minute. Add steak and mushrooms and continue cooking until steak is lightly browned, 4 to 5 minutes. Stir in milk and remaining coating mixture and continue cooking over low heat, stirring constantly, until thickened. Serve over noodles tossed with poppy seeds.

Makes 4 servings

Manhattan Turkey á la King

8 ounces wide egg noodles
1 pound boneless turkey or chicken, cut into strips
1 tablespoon vegetable oil
1 can (14½ ounces) DEL MONTE® FreshCut™ Diced Tomatoes, undrained
1 can (10¾ ounces) condensed cream of celery soup
1 medium onion, chopped
2 stalks celery, sliced
1 cup sliced mushrooms

1. Cook noodles according to package directions; drain.

2. Meanwhile, brown turkey in hot oil in large skillet over medium-high heat. Season with salt and pepper, if desired.

3. Add all remaining ingredients except noodles; cover. Reduce heat to medium. Cook 5 minutes. Remove cover; cook 5 minutes or until thickened, stirring occasionally.

4. Serve over hot noodles. Sprinkle with chopped parsley, if desired.   *Makes 6 servings*

Prep Time: 7 minutes

Cook Time: 20 minutes

Helpful Hint: Cook pasta ahead; rinse and drain. Cover and refrigerate. Just before serving, heat in microwave or dip into boiling water.

Alfredo Pasta Swirls

4 ounces uncooked fettuccini
1 package (10 ounces) frozen peas and carrots, thawed and drained
1 package (10 ounces) frozen cauliflower florets, thawed and drained
1 cup (4 ounces) shredded mozzarella cheese
1⅓ cups (2.8-ounce can) FRENCH'S® French Fried Onions, divided
1 container (10 ounces) refrigerated Alfredo sauce
½ cup milk
⅓ cup grated Parmesan cheese

Preheat oven to 375°F. Prepare pasta according to package directions using shortest cooking time. Drain; keep warm.

Combine vegetables, mozzarella cheese and ⅔ *cup* French Fried Onions in 2-quart oblong baking dish. Twirl few strands of warm fettuccini around long-tined fork to form pasta swirl. Remove pasta swirl from fork; stand upright on top of vegetable layer. Repeat to form 5 more swirls.

Combine Alfredo sauce and milk in medium bowl. Pour over pasta and vegetables. Cover loosely with foil; bake 35 minutes or until heated through. Gently stir sauce and vegetables around pasta. Top with Parmesan cheese. Sprinkle remaining ⅔ *cup* onions around pasta. Bake, uncovered, 3 minutes or until onions are golden.
                                        Makes 6 servings

Prep Time: 15 minutes
Cook Time: 38 minutes

Manhattan Turkey á la King

Four-Meat Ravioli

    Four-Meat Filling (recipe follows)
    Plum Tomato Sauce (page 52)
 4 cups all-purpose flour
¼ teaspoon salt
 2 eggs
 1 tablespoon olive oil
 1 egg yolk
 1 teaspoon milk
 1 tablespoon chopped fresh parsley
    Freshly grated Parmesan cheese
    Fresh rosemary sprig, for garnish

Prepare Four-Meat Filling; refrigerate. Prepare Plum Tomato Sauce; set aside.

For dough, mix flour and salt in large bowl. Combine 2 eggs, oil and ⅔ cup water in small bowl; whisk thoroughly. Gradually stir egg mixture into flour mixture with fork. Add additional water, 1 tablespoon at a time, to form firm but pliable dough. Place dough on lightly floured surface; flatten slightly. Knead dough 5 minutes or until smooth and elastic, adding more flour to prevent sticking if necessary. Wrap dough in plastic wrap; let rest 30 minutes.

Unwrap dough and knead briefly on lightly floured surface; divide into 4 pieces. Using lightly floured rolling pin, roll out 1 dough piece to ¹⁄₁₆-inch thickness on lightly floured surface. (Keep remaining dough pieces wrapped in plastic wrap to prevent drying.)

Cut dough into 4-inch-wide strips. Place teaspoonfuls of Four-Meat Filling along top half of long edge of each strip at 2-inch intervals.

Whisk egg yolk and milk in small bowl. Brush dough on bottom half of long edge and between filling with egg-milk mixture. Fold dough over filling; press firmly between filling and along long edge to seal, making sure all air has been pushed out. Cut ravioli apart with fluted pastry wheel. Repeat with remaining 3 dough pieces, filling and egg-milk mixture.

Cook ravioli, ¼ at a time, in large saucepan of boiling salted water 3 to 5 minutes just until tender. Remove with slotted spoon; drain well. Add ravioli to reserved sauce. Bring sauce and ravioli to a boil over medium-high heat; reduce heat to medium-low. Simmer, uncovered, 6 to 8 minutes until heated through. Sprinkle with parsley and cheese. Garnish, if desired. Serve immediately. *Makes 6 servings*

Four-Meat Filling

 2 small boneless skinless chicken breast
    halves (about 4 ounces each), cooked
 5 ounces fresh spinach, cooked and squeezed
    dry
 3 ounces prosciutto or cooked ham
1½ ounces hard salami
 1 clove garlic
 6 ounces ground beef
½ cup chopped fresh parsley
 2 eggs
¼ teaspoon ground allspice
¼ teaspoon salt

Mince chicken, spinach, prosciutto, salami and garlic; combine in medium bowl with beef, parsley, eggs, allspice and salt. Mix well.

(continued on page 52)

Four-Meat Ravioli

(Four-Meat Ravioli continued)

Plum Tomato Sauce

⅓ cup butter or margarine
1 clove garlic, minced
1 can (28 ounces) Italian plum tomatoes, undrained
1 can (8 ounces) tomato sauce
¾ teaspoon salt
½ teaspoon ground allspice
½ teaspoon dried basil leaves
½ teaspoon dried rosemary leaves
⅛ teaspoon black pepper

Heat butter in large saucepan over medium heat until melted and bubbly; cook and stir garlic in hot butter 30 seconds. Press tomatoes and juice through sieve into garlic mixture; discard seeds. Stir in tomato sauce, salt, allspice, basil, rosemary and black pepper. Cover and simmer 30 minutes. Uncover and simmer 15 minutes more or until sauce thickens, stirring occasionally.

Fettuccine with Ham & Mushroom Sauce

¼ cup butter or margarine
8 ounces fresh mushrooms, sliced, or 1 can (8 ounces) sliced mushrooms, drained
1 medium onion, chopped
1 pound cooked ham, chopped
1 recipe White Sauce Base (recipe follows)
¼ cup (1 ounce) grated Parmesan cheese
8 ounces fettuccine noodles, cooked and drained

In large skillet, melt butter over medium heat. Add mushrooms and onion; cook and stir 5 minutes or until tender. Add ham; mix well.

Prepare White Sauce Base. Stir in Parmesan cheese; pour over ham mixture. Heat until bubbly, stirring frequently. Serve over hot noodles. Garnish with chopped fresh parsley and additional grated Parmesan cheese, if desired.

Makes 4 servings

White Sauce Base

2 tablespoons butter or margarine
2 tablespoons all-purpose flour
¼ teaspoon salt
½ teaspoon TABASCO® pepper sauce
1¼ cups milk

In small saucepan, melt butter over low heat. Blend in flour, salt and TABASCO® sauce. Gradually stir in milk. Bring to a boil over medium heat, stirring constantly. Simmer 1 minute.

Makes about 1 cup

Microwave: In 1-quart microwave-safe bowl, melt butter on HIGH 30 to 45 seconds. Stir in flour. Microwave, uncovered, on HIGH 30 seconds or until bubbly. Gradually stir in milk, salt and TABASCO® sauce. Microwave, uncovered, on HIGH 2½ to 3½ minutes, until thickened, stirring every minute.

Traditional Spaghetti & Meatballs

1 pound Spaghetti, Linguine or Thin
   Spaghetti, uncooked

MEATBALLS
   4 slices white bread
   ½ cup skim milk
   2 large egg whites
   8 ounces ground turkey
   8 ounces extra-lean ground beef
   ¼ cup grated Romano cheese
   1 teaspoon dried basil
   ½ teaspoon dried oregano
   ½ teaspoon salt
   ¼ teaspoon pepper

SAUCE
   1 recipe Basic Tomato Sauce (recipe follows)
   1 teaspoon vegetable oil, divided

Place bread in medium mixing bowl; pour milk over bread. Let soak 5 minutes. Add egg whites, ground turkey, ground beef, Romano cheese, basil, oregano, salt and pepper. Knead mixture until it is smooth. To prevent sticking, dip your hands into cool water before forming each meatball. Form mixture into 30 (1½-inch) balls.

Bring tomato sauce to a simmer over low heat in large, heavy saucepan. Heat ½ teaspoon vegetable oil in large nonstick skillet. Add half the meatballs to skillet and cook until browned. Spoon cooked meatballs into tomato sauce. Repeat with remaining oil and meatballs. Add to tomato sauce. Simmer, stirring, 20 minutes.

Prepare pasta according to package directions; drain. Transfer to large serving bowl; remove bay leaves. Pour over pasta; serve.

Makes 6 servings

Basic Tomato Sauce

   1 teaspoon vegetable oil
   1 medium onion, chopped
   2 cloves garlic, chopped
   2 (28 ounce) cans whole tomatoes
   1 (6 ounce) can tomato paste
   2 teaspoons dried Italian seasoning
   2 bay leaves

In medium, heavy saucepan stir oil, onion and garlic. Cook over low heat, stirring often, about 6 to 8 minutes or until onion is very soft.

In food processor or blender, purée tomatoes. Add tomatoes, tomato paste, Italian seasoning and bay leaves to onions and bring to simmer over medium-high heat. Reduce heat to very low; let sauce simmer 30 minutes, stirring the bottom often to prevent burning. If you are adding meatballs, do so at this time, and simmer 20 minutes, stirring often. If you are not adding meatballs, simmer sauce 20 minutes (50 minutes total). Season to taste with salt and pepper. Remove bay leaves before serving.

Makes 4 servings

Favorite recipe from **National Pasta Association**

Pasta Pizza

1 pound Ziti, Rigatoni or other medium
    pasta shape, uncooked
1 tablespoon olive or vegetable oil
1 tablespoon dried mixed Italian herbs *or*
    2 tablespoons minced fresh oregano *plus*
    2 tablespoons minced fresh parsley
1 (8-ounce) can tomato sauce
¼ cup grated Romano cheese
2 cloves garlic, minced
1 teaspoon hot red pepper flakes (optional)
1 (16-ounce) can crushed tomatoes *or* 2
    cups chopped fresh tomatoes
1 green bell pepper, ribs and seeds removed,
    chopped
½ cup chopped carrots
1 can chick-peas, rinsed and drained
6 green olives, sliced
1 cup shredded part-skim mozzarella cheese

Prepare pasta according to package directions,
reducing cooking time by 1 to 2 minutes; drain.

Preheat oven to 400°F. Spray 13×9×2-inch
baking dish with vegetable cooking spray.
Transfer pasta to baking dish and toss with oil,
mixed herbs, tomato sauce and Romano cheese.
Mix garlic and hot red pepper flakes with
tomatoes and pour over top of pasta. Layer
remaining ingredients, ending with mozzarella.
Bake 15 minutes or until center is warm and
cheese is melted. Serve immediately.

Makes 6 to 8 servings

Favorite recipe from **National Pasta Association**

Cheeseburger Macaroni

1 cup mostaccioli or elbow macaroni,
    uncooked
1 pound ground beef
1 medium onion, chopped
1 can (14½ ounces) DEL MONTE®
    Original or Italian Recipe Stewed
    Tomatoes
¼ cup DEL MONTE® Tomato Ketchup
1 cup (4 ounces) shredded Cheddar cheese

1. Cook pasta according to package directions;
drain.

2. Brown beef with onion in large skillet; drain.
Season with salt and pepper, if desired. Stir in
tomatoes, ketchup and pasta; heat through.

3. Top with cheese. Garnish, if desired.

Makes 4 servings

Prep Time: 8 minutes
Cook Time: 15 minutes

Cheeseburger Macaroni

Macaroni and Cheese with Tomatoes

8 ounces Elbow Macaroni, uncooked
2 tablespoons butter or margarine
1 tablespoon all-purpose flour
¼ teaspoon dry mustard
½ teaspoon salt
2 cups skim milk
2 cups shredded hard cheese (such as
    Cheddar)
2 ripe tomatoes, sliced into ½-inch-thick
    slices
½ cup fresh bread crumbs

Prepare pasta according to package directions; drain. Preheat oven to 375°F.

In 2-quart saucepan over medium heat, melt butter. Add flour, dry mustard and salt; cook 2 to 3 minutes. Add milk, a little at a time, and continue stirring until mixture thickens. Add cheese and stir until melted.

Place 2 tomato slices in bottom of baking pan. Top with half of the pasta. Top with another two slices of tomato and remaining pasta. Pour sauce over all. Arrange three slices of tomato on top; sprinkle with bread crumbs. Bake 20 minutes. Serve immediately.   *Makes 4 servings*

Favorite recipe from **National Pasta Association**

Hot Dog Macaroni

1 package (8 ounces) hot dogs
1 cup uncooked corkscrew pasta
1 cup shredded Cheddar cheese
1 box (10 ounces) BIRDS EYE® frozen
    Green Peas
1 cup 1% milk

• Slice hot dogs into bite-size pieces; set aside.

• In large saucepan, cook pasta according to package directions; drain and return to saucepan.

• Stir in hot dogs, cheese, peas and milk. Cook over medium heat 10 minutes or until cheese is melted, stirring occasionally.   *Makes 4 servings*

Prep Time: 10 minutes
Cook Time: 20 minutes

Salsa Mac 'n Cheese

1 pound ground beef
1 jar (16 ounces) chunky salsa
1½ cups water
1 package (7 ounces) elbow macaroni
¾ pound (12 ounces) VELVEETA® Process
    Cheese Spread, cut up

Brown beef in large skillet; drain. Add salsa and water. Bring to a boil. Stir in macaroni. Reduce heat to medium-low; cover. Simmer 8 to 10 minutes or until macaroni are tender. Add VELVEETA; stir until melted.

Makes 4 to 6 servings

Hot Dog Macaroni

Chicken Tortellini with Mushroom-Cream Sauce

2 cups plus 1 tablespoon all-purpose flour
½ teaspoon salt, divided
4 eggs, divided
1 tablespoon milk
1 teaspoon olive oil
2 small boneless skinless chicken breast
   halves (about 4 ounces each), cooked
   and minced
2 ounces fresh spinach, cooked, squeezed
   dry and minced
2 ounces prosciutto or cooked ham, minced
⅓ cup plus 2 tablespoons grated Parmesan
   cheese, divided
2 cups heavy or whipping cream, divided
   Dash black pepper
3 tablespoons butter or margarine
½ pound fresh mushrooms, thinly sliced
3 tablespoons chopped fresh parsley

Combine flour and ¼ teaspoon salt on pastry board or cutting board; make well in center. Whisk 3 eggs, milk and oil in small bowl until well blended; gradually pour into well in flour mixture while mixing with fingertips or fork to form ball of dough. Place dough on lightly floured surface; flatten slightly. Knead dough 5 minutes or until smooth and elastic, adding more flour to prevent sticking if necessary. Wrap dough in plastic wrap; set aside. Allow dough to stand at least 15 minutes.

Combine chicken, spinach, prosciutto and remaining egg in medium bowl. Add 2 tablespoons cheese, 1 tablespoon cream, remaining ¼ teaspoon salt and pepper to spinach mixture; mix well.

Unwrap dough and knead briefly on lightly floured surface; divide into 3 pieces. Using lightly floured rolling pin, roll out 1 dough piece to ¹⁄₁₆-inch thickness on lightly floured surface. (Keep remaining dough pieces wrapped in plastic wrap to prevent drying.)

Cut out dough circles with 2-inch round cutter. Cover rolled dough with clean kitchen towel to prevent drying while working. Place ½ teaspoon chicken filling in center of 1 dough circle; brush edge of circle lightly with water. Fold circle in half to enclose filling, making sure all air has been pushed out. Pinch outside edges together firmly to seal. Brush end of half circle with water; wrap around finger, overlapping ends. Pinch to seal. Place tortellini on clean kitchen towel. Repeat with remaining dough circles, rerolling dough scraps as needed. Repeat with remaining 2 dough pieces and chicken filling. Let tortellini dry on towel 30 minutes.

Heat butter in 3-quart saucepan over medium heat until melted and bubbly; cook and stir mushrooms in hot butter 3 minutes. Stir in remaining cream. Bring to a boil over medium heat; reduce heat to low. Simmer, uncovered, 3 minutes. Stir in remaining ⅓ cup cheese; cook and stir 1 minute. Remove from heat.

Cook tortellini, ⅓ at a time, in large saucepan of boiling salted water 2 to 3 minutes just until tender. Drain well; add to cream sauce. Bring *just* to a boil over medium heat; reduce heat to low. Simmer 2 minutes. Sprinkle with parsley. Serve immediately.   *Makes 6 to 8 servings*

Chicken Tortellini with Mushroom-Cream Sauce

Delicious Ground Beef Medley

1 pound ground beef
½ cup chopped onion
¼ cup chopped celery
2 cups uncooked elbow macaroni
1 can (10¾ ounces) condensed cream of chicken soup
1 can (10¾ ounces) condensed cream of mushroom soup
⅔ cup milk
½ teaspoon salt
    Dash of pepper
½ cup chopped green bell pepper
1 can (16 ounces) whole kernel corn, drained

1. Preheat oven to 350°F. Brown ground beef, onion and celery. Drain.

2. Cook macaroni according to package directions; drain.

3. Combine soups, milk, salt and pepper in 2½-quart casserole. Add ground beef, macaroni, bell pepper and corn. Bake for 30 minutes.

Makes 8 servings

Favorite recipe from **North Dakota Beef Commission**

Tuna Mac and Cheese

1 package (7¼ ounces) macaroni and cheese dinner
1 can (12 ounces) STARKIST® Solid White or Chunk Light Tuna, drained and chunked
1 cup frozen peas
½ cup shredded Cheddar cheese
½ cup milk
1 teaspoon Italian herb seasoning
¼ teaspoon garlic powder (optional)
1 tablespoon grated Parmesan cheese

Prepare macaroni and cheese dinner according to package directions. Add remaining ingredients except Parmesan cheese. Pour into 1½-quart microwavable serving dish. Cover with vented plastic wrap; microwave on HIGH 2 minutes. Stir; continue heating on HIGH 2½ to 3½ more minutes or until cheese is melted and mixture is heated through. Sprinkle with Parmesan cheese.

Makes 5 to 6 servings

Prep Time: 20 minutes

Veggie Ravioli

2 cans (15 ounces each) ravioli
1 bag (16 ounces) BIRDS EYE® frozen
   Mixed Vegetables
2 cups shredded mozzarella cheese

• In 1½-quart microwave-safe casserole dish,
combine ravioli and vegetables.

• Cover; microwave on HIGH 10 minutes,
stirring halfway through cook time.

• Uncover; sprinkle with cheese. Microwave
5 minutes more or until cheese is melted.
Makes 6 servings

Prep Time: 5 minutes
Cook Time: 15 minutes

Serving Suggestion: Sprinkle with grated
Parmesan cheese.

Mushroom and Tuna Bake

1 can (10¾ ounces) cream of celery soup
1 cup milk
1 jar (4 ounces) sliced mushrooms, drained
½ cup grated Parmesan cheese, divided
1 teaspoon dried Italian herb blend
½ teaspoon seasoned salt
⅛ to ¼ teaspoon garlic powder
1 can (12 ounces) STARKIST® Solid White
   or Chunk Light Tuna, drained and
   chunked
3 cups cooked egg noodles
1 cup crispy rice cereal

In medium saucepan, combine soup and milk;
blend well. Add mushrooms, ¼ cup cheese,
Italian herb blend, seasoned salt, garlic powder
and tuna; cook over low heat until heated
through. Remove from heat; stir in egg noodles.
Transfer mixture to lightly greased 11×7-inch
baking dish. Top with remaining ¼ cup Parmesan
cheese and cereal. Bake in 350°F oven 30
minutes. *Makes 6 servings*

Prep Time: 40 minutes

Pasta Picadillo

12 ounces uncooked medium shell pasta
1 pound lean ground sirloin
²⁄₃ cup finely chopped green bell pepper
½ cup finely chopped onion
2 cloves garlic, minced
1 can (8-ounces) tomato sauce
⅓ cup raisins
3 tablespoons sliced pimiento-stuffed green
   olives
2 tablespoons drained capers
2 tablespoons vinegar
½ teaspoon black pepper
¼ teaspoon salt

1. Cook pasta according to package directions. Drain; set aside.

2. Spray large nonstick skillet with nonstick cooking spray. Add beef, bell pepper, onion and garlic. Brown beef mixture over medium-high heat 5 minutes or until no longer pink, stirring to separate beef; drain fat. Stir in tomato sauce, ½ cup water, raisins, olives, capers, vinegar, pepper and salt. Reduce heat to medium-low; cook, covered, 15 minutes, stirring occasionally.

3. Add pasta to skillet; toss to coat. Cover and heat through, about 2 minutes.

Makes 6 (1-cup) servings

Macaroni Italiano

1 can (16 ounces) tomatoes, undrained
½ teaspoon baking soda
1 can (8 ounces) tomato sauce
1¼ cups low-fat cottage cheese
¼ cup grated Parmesan cheese
1 package (10 ounces) frozen chopped
   spinach, thawed and squeezed dry
1½ cups frozen peas, thawed
1 teaspoon dried basil leaves, crushed
½ teaspoon black pepper
8 ounces elbow macaroni, cooked according
   to package directions and drained
¾ cup chopped toasted California walnuts*
2 tablespoons chopped fresh parsley
   Salt

*Toasting is optional.

Preheat oven to 350°F. Oil 2½-quart baking pan.

Place tomatoes and juice in large bowl. Add baking soda; break up tomatoes into small chunks with fork. Stir in tomato sauce. Add cottage cheese, Parmesan cheese, spinach, peas, basil and black pepper. Mix well. Add macaroni to cheese mixture; mix to coat thoroughly. Pour into prepared baking pan.

Cover with foil; bake 20 minutes. Uncover; bake 10 minutes. Stir in walnuts and sprinkle with parsley. Season with salt to taste.

Makes 6 servings

Favorite recipe from **Walnut Marketing Board**

Pasta Picadillo

Tetrazzini Pasta Supper

6 quarts salted water
1 package (16 ounces) tubular pasta, such
  as ziti or penne
2 tablespoons butter or margarine
3 green onions, minced
2 cloves garlic, minced
1 pound fresh shiitake mushrooms, stems
  removed and caps sliced, or fresh
  domestic mushrooms, sliced
3 tablespoons dry sherry
½ teaspoon dried tarragon leaves
  Salt and ground black pepper
2 to 3 cups coarsely chopped cooked
  PERDUE® Chicken or Turkey
1½ cups part-skim ricotta cheese
¾ cup freshly grated Parmesan cheese

In large saucepan over high heat, bring water to
boil. Cook pasta according to package directions
until tender. Reserve 1 cup cooking water from
pasta. Drain pasta and place in large serving bowl.

Meanwhile, in large skillet over low heat, melt
butter. Add green onions and garlic; cook about
1 minute or until tender, stirring constantly.
Increase heat to high; add mushrooms, sherry,
tarragon and ¼ teaspoon *each* salt and pepper.
Cook about 5 minutes or until liquid is evaporated
and mushrooms are browned, stirring constantly.
Add chicken; cook 1 minute longer or until
heated through.

To serve, pour warm chicken mixture over hot
pasta. Add ricotta and Parmesan cheeses with
about ⅓ cup reserved hot cooking water. Toss
and add additional cooking water, if necessary, to
make a creamy sauce. Season with additional salt
and pepper; serve immediately.

Makes 4 to 6 servings

Western Wagon Wheels

1 pound lean ground beef or ground turkey
2 cups uncooked wagon wheel pasta
1 can (14½ ounces) stewed tomatoes
1½ cups water
1 box (10 ounces) BIRDS EYE® frozen
  Sweet Corn
½ cup barbecue sauce

• In large skillet, cook beef over medium heat
5 minutes or until well browned.

• Stir in pasta, tomatoes, water, corn and
barbecue sauce; bring to boil.

• Reduce heat to low; cover and simmer
15 to 20 minutes or until pasta is tender, stirring
occasionally. Add salt and pepper to taste.

Makes 4 servings

Prep Time: 5 minutes

Cook Time: 25 minutes

Serving Suggestion: Serve with corn bread or
corn muffins.

Western Wagon Wheels

Sausage Spaghetti

1 pound BOB EVANS FARMS® Original Recipe or Italian Roll Sausage
1 large onion, chopped
2 cloves garlic, minced
1 (6-ounce) can tomato paste
1 (32-ounce) can whole tomatoes (regular or Italian style), undrained
1 (4-ounce) can mushroom stems and pieces, drained
1 tablespoon Worcestershire sauce
2 tablespoons Italian seasoning, or to taste
1 pound spaghetti, cooked according to package directions and drained
Grated Parmesan cheese

Crumble sausage into large skillet. Add onion and garlic. Cook over medium heat until sausage is browned, stirring occasionally. Drain off any drippings. Stir in tomato paste; cook 3 minutes. Add all remaining ingredients except spaghetti and cheese, stirring well to break up tomatoes. Bring to a boil over high heat. Reduce heat to low; simmer 30 minutes, stirring occasionally. Adjust seasonings, if desired. Pour over hot spaghetti. Serve with cheese. Refrigerate leftovers. *Makes 6 servings*

Serving Suggestion: Serve the sauce hot over any type of pasta.

Western Skillet Noodles

1 pound ground beef
2⅓ cups water
1 package LIPTON® Noodles & Sauce— Beef Flavor
2 teaspoons chili powder
1 can (12 ounces) whole kernel corn with sweet peppers, drained
1 cup shredded cheddar cheese (about 4 ounces), divided

In 10-inch skillet, brown beef; drain. Add water and bring to a boil; stir in noodles & sauce— beef flavor and chili powder. Continue boiling over medium heat, stirring occasionally, 7 minutes. Add corn and ⅔ cup cheese. Simmer 5 minutes or until cheese is melted. Top with remaining ⅓ cup cheese.

Makes about 4 servings

Lasagna Italiano

1½ pounds ground beef
½ cup chopped onion
1 (14½-ounce) can tomatoes, cut up
1 (6-ounce) can tomato paste
⅓ cup water
1 garlic clove, minced
1 teaspoon dried oregano leaves, crushed
¼ teaspoon black pepper
6 ounces lasagna noodles, cooked, drained
2 (6-ounce) packages KRAFT® Natural
    Low-Moisture Part-Skim Mozzarella
    Cheese Slices
½ pound VELVEETA® Pasteurized Process
    Cheese Spread, thinly sliced
½ cup (2 ounces) KRAFT® 100% Grated
    Parmesan Cheese

In large skillet, brown meat; drain. Add onion; cook until tender. Stir in tomatoes, tomato paste, water, garlic and seasonings. Cover; simmer 30 minutes. In 12×8-inch baking dish, layer half of noodles, meat sauce, mozzarella cheese, process cheese spread and Parmesan cheese; repeat layers. Bake at 350°F 30 minutes. Let stand 10 minutes before serving.   *Makes 6 to 8 servings*

Prep Time: 40 minutes
Bake Time: 30 minutes plus standing

Ravioli Stew

2 tablespoons olive or vegetable oil
1 medium onion, chopped
2 medium carrots, diced
2 ribs celery, diced
1 medium green bell pepper, chopped
1 clove garlic, finely chopped*
1 can (15 to 19 ounces) red kidney beans,
    rinsed and drained
4 plum tomatoes, chopped
1 envelope LIPTON® Recipe Secrets
    Golden Herb with Lemon Soup Mix
2½ cups water
1 package (8 or 10 ounces) refrigerated
    cheese ravioli
Grated Parmesan cheese (optional)

*Also terrific with LIPTON® Recipe Secrets Savory Herb with Garlic Soup Mix.

*If using LIPTON® Recipe Secrets Savory Herb with Garlic Soup Mix, omit garlic.

In Dutch oven or 6-quart saucepot, heat oil over medium heat and cook onion, carrots, celery, green pepper and garlic, stirring occasionally, 5 minutes or until tender. Stir in beans, tomatoes and golden herb with lemon soup mix blended with water. Bring to a boil over high heat. Stir in ravioli. Reduce heat to medium and cook, stirring gently, 5 minutes or until ravioli are tender. Serve, if desired, with grated Parmesan cheese.
Makes about 4 (2-cup) servings

Tacos in Pasta Shells

18 uncooked jumbo pasta shells
2 tablespoons butter, melted
1¼ pounds ground beef
1 package (3 ounces) cream cheese with chives, cut into ½ inch pieces, softened
1 teaspoon salt
1 teaspoon chili powder
1 cup prepared taco sauce
1 cup (4 ounces) shredded Cheddar cheese
1 cup (4 ounces) shredded Monterey Jack cheese
1½ cups crushed tortilla chips
1 cup sour cream
3 green onions, chopped

1. Cook pasta according to package directions; drain well. Return to saucepan. Toss shells with butter.

2. Preheat oven to 350°F. Butter 13×9-inch baking pan.

3. Cook beef in large skillet over medium-high heat until brown, stirring to separate meat; drain drippings. Reduce heat to medium-low. Add cream cheese, salt and chili powder; simmer 5 minutes.

4. Fill shells with beef mixture. Arrange shells in prepared pan. Pour taco sauce over shells. Cover with foil.

5. Bake 15 minutes. Uncover; top with Cheddar cheese, Monterey Jack cheese and chips. Bake 15 minutes or until bubbly. Top with sour cream and onions. Garnish, if desired.

Makes 4 to 6 servings

Veggie Tuna Pasta

1 package (16 ounces) medium pasta shells
1 bag (16 ounces) BIRDS EYE® frozen Farm Fresh Mixtures Broccoli, Corn & Red Peppers
1 can (10 ounces) chunky light tuna, packed in water
1 can (10¾ ounces) reduced-fat cream of mushroom soup

• In large saucepan, cook pasta according to package directions. Add vegetables during last 10 minutes; drain and return to saucepan.

• Stir in tuna and soup. Add salt and pepper to taste. Cook over medium heat until heated through. *Makes 4 servings*

Prep Time: 2 minutes
Cook Time: 12 to 15 minutes

Variation: Stir in 1 can (4 to 6 ounces) chopped ripe olives with tuna.

Serving Suggestion: For a creamier dish, add a few tablespoons water; blend well.

Classic

COUNTRY CASSEROLES

Italian Three-Cheese Macaroni

2 cups uncooked elbow macaroni
4 tablespoons margarine or butter
3 tablespoons all-purpose flour
1 teaspoon dried Italian seasoning
½ to 1 teaspoon black pepper
½ teaspoon salt
2 cups milk
¾ cup (3 ounces) shredded Cheddar cheese
¼ cup grated Parmesan cheese
1 can (14½ ounces) diced tomatoes, drained
1 cup (4 ounces) shredded mozzarella cheese
½ cup dry bread crumbs
Fresh chives and oregano sprig

Preheat oven to 350°F. Spray 2-quart round casserole with nonstick cooking spray.

Cook pasta according to package directions. Drain; set aside.

Meanwhile, melt margarine in medium saucepan over medium heat. Add flour, Italian seasoning, pepper and salt, stirring until smooth. Gradually add milk, stirring constantly until slightly thickened. Add Cheddar and Parmesan cheeses; stir until cheeses melt.

Layer pasta, tomatoes and cheese sauce in prepared casserole. Repeat layers.

Combine mozzarella cheese and bread crumbs in small bowl. Sprinkle evenly over casserole. Spray bread crumb mixture several times with cooking spray.

Bake, covered, 30 minutes or until hot and bubbly. Uncover; bake 5 minutes or until top is golden brown. Garnish with chives and oregano, if desired.   *Makes 4 servings*

Italian Three-Cheese Macaroni

Curly Macaroni Pie

1 pound uncooked rotini pasta
1 cup seasoned dry bread crumbs
½ cup (2 ounces) grated ALPINE LACE®
    Fat Free Pasteurized Process Skim Milk
    Cheese Product—For Parmesan Lovers
½ cup packed fresh parsley
2 tablespoons unsalted butter substitute,
    melted
1½ cups chopped red onions
1½ cups coarsely chopped red bell peppers
2 cups (8 ounces) shredded ALPINE
    LACE® Reduced Fat Swiss Cheese
2 cups (8 ounces) shredded ALPINE
    LACE® American Flavor Pasteurized
    Process Cheese Product with Jalapeño
    Peppers
2½ cups 2% low fat milk
2 tablespoons Dijon mustard

1. Preheat the oven to 350°F. Spray a 14-inch oval or round ovenproof baking dish and a large nonstick skillet with nonstick cooking spray. Cook the rotini according to package directions just until al dente. Drain well, place in the baking dish and keep warm.

2. In a food processor, place the bread crumbs, Parmesan, parsley and butter. Process 1 minute or until finely chopped; set aside.

3. Heat the skillet over medium-high heat for 1 minute. Add the onions and bell peppers and sauté for 5 minutes or until soft. Sprinkle over the rotini in the baking dish. Sprinkle with 1½ cups of the bread crumb mixture and the Swiss and pepper cheeses; toss to mix well.

4. In a measuring cup, whisk together the milk and mustard; fold into the rotini mixture until well coated. Top with the remaining bread crumb mixture. Sprinkle with paprika, if you wish. Cover tightly with foil and bake for 50 minutes or until bubbly. Remove the foil and bake 5 minutes more. Transfer to a rack and let stand for 15 minutes. Garnish the pie with fresh parsley leaves, if you wish. Serve hot or warm. *Makes 14 servings*

Macaroni and Cheese Dijon

1¼ cups milk
12 ounces pasteurized process Cheddar
  cheese spread, cubed
½ cup GREY POUPON® Dijon Mustard
⅓ cup sliced green onions
6 slices bacon, cooked and crumbled
⅛ teaspoon ground red pepper
12 ounces tri-color rotelle or spiral-shaped
  pasta, cooked
1 (2.8-ounce) can French fried onion rings

In medium saucepan, over low heat, heat milk, cheese and mustard until cheese melts and mixture is smooth. Stir in green onions, bacon and pepper; remove from heat.

In large bowl, combine hot pasta and cheese mixture, tossing until well coated; spoon into greased 2-quart casserole. Cover; bake at 350°F for 15 to 20 minutes. Uncover; stir. Top with onion rings. Bake, uncovered, for 5 minutes more. Let stand 10 minutes before serving. Garnish as desired.   *Makes 6 servings*

Chicken Noodle Tetrazzini

12 ounces Medium Egg Noodles, uncooked
2 tablespoons margarine
2 tablespoons all-purpose flour
1½ cups skim milk
1 cup water
2 chicken-flavored bouillon cubes
⅛ teaspoon black pepper
⅛ teaspoon ground red pepper
1 (10-ounce package) frozen peas, thawed
½ cup nonfat plain yogurt
4 tablespoons grated Parmesan cheese,
  divided
8 ounces fresh mushrooms, sliced
2 cups diced cooked chicken

Prepare egg noodles according to package directions. While noodles are cooking, melt margarine in medium saucepan. Blend in flour until smooth. Stir in milk, water, bouillon cubes, black pepper and red pepper. Cook over medium heat about 10 minutes, stirring constantly, until mixture thickens and comes to a boil. Stir in peas, yogurt and 2 tablespoons Parmesan cheese.

Preheat oven to 425°F. When noodles are done, drain well. Combine noodles, mushrooms, sauce and chicken in large bowl. Turn mixture into lightly greased 12×9-inch baking dish. Sprinkle with remaining Parmesan. Bake 15 minutes. Serve immediately.   *Makes 4 servings*

Favorite recipe from **National Pasta Association**

Macaroni and Cheese Dijon

Baked Pasta and Cheese Supreme

8 ounces uncooked fusilli pasta
8 ounces uncooked bacon, diced
½ onion, chopped
2 cloves garlic, minced
2 teaspoons dried oregano, divided
1 can (8 ounces) tomato sauce
1 teaspoon hot pepper sauce (optional)
1½ cups (6 ounces) shredded Cheddar or
    Colby cheese
½ cup fresh bread crumbs (from 1 slice of
    white bread)
1 tablespoon melted butter
    Yellow pear tomatoes and basil leaves for
    garnish

1. Preheat oven to 400°F. Cook pasta according to package directions; drain.

2. Meanwhile, cook bacon in large ovenproof skillet over medium heat until crisp; drain.

3. Add onion, garlic and 1 teaspoon oregano to skillet; cook and stir about 3 minutes or until onion is tender. Stir in tomato sauce and hot pepper sauce, if desired. Add cooked pasta and cheese to skillet; stir to coat.

4. Combine bread crumbs, remaining 1 teaspoon oregano and melted butter in small bowl; sprinkle over pasta mixture. Bake about 5 minutes or until hot and bubbly. Garnish, if desired.

Makes 4 servings

Country-Style Lasagna

9 lasagna noodles (2 inches wide)
2 cans (14½ ounces each) DEL MONTE®
    Italian Recipe Stewed Tomatoes
  Milk
2 tablespoons butter or margarine
3 tablespoons all-purpose flour
1 teaspoon dried basil, crushed
1 cup diced cooked ham
2 cups (8 ounces) shredded mozzarella cheese

1. Cook noodles according to package directions; rinse, drain and separate noodles.

2. Meanwhile, drain tomatoes, reserving liquid; pour liquid into measuring cup. Add milk to measure 2 cups.

3. In large saucepan, melt butter; stir in flour and basil. Cook over medium heat 3 minutes, stirring constantly. Stir in reserved liquid; cook until thickened, stirring constantly. Season to taste with salt and pepper, if desired. Stir in tomatoes.

4. Spread thin layer of sauce on bottom of 11×7-inch or 2-quart baking dish. Top with 3 noodles and ⅓ *each* of sauce, ham and cheese; repeat layers twice, ending with cheese.

5. Bake, uncovered, at 375°F 25 minutes. Serve with grated Parmesan cheese and garnish, if desired.

Makes 6 servings

Prep Time: 15 minutes
Cook Time: 25 minutes

Baked Pasta and Cheese Supreme

Three Cheese Vegetable Lasagna

1 large onion, chopped
3 cloves garlic, minced
1 teaspoon olive oil
1 can (28 ounces) no-salt-added tomato
    purée
1 can (14½ ounces) no-salt-added tomatoes,
    undrained and chopped
2 cups (6 ounces) sliced fresh mushrooms
1 zucchini, diced
1 large green bell pepper, chopped
2 teaspoons basil, crushed
1 teaspoon *each* salt and sugar (optional)
½ teaspoon *each* red pepper flakes and
    oregano, crushed
2 cups (15 ounces) SARGENTO® Light
    Ricotta Cheese
1 package (10 ounces) frozen chopped
    spinach, thawed and squeezed dry
2 egg whites
2 tablespoons (½ ounce) SARGENTO®
    Fancy Supreme® Shredded Parmesan
    Cheese
½ pound lasagna noodles, cooked according
    to package directions, without oil or salt
¾ cup (3 ounces) *each* SARGENTO®
    Preferred Light® Fancy Shredded
    Mozzarella and Mild Cheddar Cheese,
    divided

Spray large skillet with nonstick vegetable spray. Add onion, garlic and olive oil; cook over medium heat until tender, stirring occasionally.

Add tomato purée, tomatoes with liquid, mushrooms, zucchini, bell pepper, basil, salt, sugar, pepper flakes and oregano. Heat to a boil. Reduce heat; cover and simmer 10 minutes or until vegetables are crisp-tender.

Combine Ricotta cheese, spinach, egg whites and Parmesan cheese; mix well and set aside.

Spread 1 cup sauce in bottom of 13×9-inch baking dish. Layer 3 lasagna noodles over sauce. Top with half of Ricotta cheese mixture and 2 cups sauce. Repeat layering with 3 more lasagna noodles, remaining Ricotta mixture and 2 cups sauce.

Combine Mozzarella and Cheddar cheeses. Sprinkle ¾ cup cheese mixture over sauce. Top with remaining lasagna noodles and sauce. Cover with foil; bake at 375°F 30 minutes. Uncover; bake 15 minutes more. Sprinkle with remaining ¾ cup cheese mixture. Let stand 10 minutes before serving. *Makes 10 servings*

Three Cheese Vegetable Lasagna

Crazy Lasagna Casserole

1½ pounds ground beef or turkey
1 teaspoon LAWRY'S® Seasoned Salt
1 package (1.5 ounces) LAWRY'S®
Original-Style Spaghetti Sauce Spices
& Seasonings
1 can (8 ounces) tomato sauce
1 can (6 ounces) tomato paste
1½ cups water
1 package (10 ounces) medium-size shell
macaroni, cooked and drained
1 carton (16 ounces) small curd cottage
cheese
1½ cups (6 ounces) shredded Cheddar cheese

In large skillet, brown beef until crumbly; drain fat. Add Seasoned Salt, Original-Style Spaghetti Sauce Spices & Seasonings, tomato sauce, tomato paste and water; blend well. Bring to a boil over medium high heat. Reduce heat and simmer, uncovered, 10 minutes, stirring occasionally.

In shallow 2-quart casserole, layer half of macaroni, cottage cheese and meat sauce. Sprinkle ½ cup Cheddar cheese over meat sauce. Repeat layers, ending with remaining meat sauce. Top with remaining 1 cup Cheddar cheese. Bake, uncovered, in 350°F oven 30 to 40 minutes or until bubbly and cheese is melted.

Makes 8 servings

Chicken & Mushroom Noodle Marsala

12 ounces Medium Egg Noodles, uncooked
1 egg white
1½ pounds boneless skinless chicken breasts,
cut crosswise into ½-inch pieces
⅓ cup Italian seasoned dry bread crumbs
¼ cup grated Parmesan cheese
2 tablespoons olive oil, divided
2 (4-ounce packages) mixed exotic
mushrooms or 1 (8-ounce package)
sliced mushrooms
4 cloves garlic, minced or 2 teaspoons
bottled minced garlic
¼ teaspoon salt (optional)
¼ teaspoon freshly ground black pepper
1 cup canned low-sodium chicken broth
4 teaspoons cornstarch
1 cup dry marsala wine
3 tablespoons chopped fresh basil or parsley

Cook pasta according to package directions. While pasta is cooking, beat egg white in large bowl. Add chicken to egg white; toss to coat. Sprinkle with bread crumbs and cheese; toss well.

Heat 1 tablespoon oil in large nonstick skillet over medium-high heat until hot. Add half of chicken; sauté 3 to 4 minutes or until chicken is no longer pink. Transfer to plate; keep warm. Repeat with remaining 1 tablespoon oil and remaining half of chicken.

Cook mushrooms and garlic in same skillet 3 minutes over medium heat. Sprinkle with salt, if desired, and pepper. Combine broth and cornstarch in medium bowl; stir in wine; add to skillet. Increase heat to medium-high and bring to a simmer. Simmer, uncovered, 2 to 3 minutes or until sauce thickens, stirring occasionally.

Drain noodles; toss with chicken. Divide evenly among 6 serving plates. Spoon mushroom sauce over pasta mixture; sprinkle with basil. Serve with additional basil, if desired.

Makes 6 servings

Favorite recipe from **National Pasta Association**

Chicken Pot Pie Lasagne

    12 pieces Lasagne, uncooked
     1 pound boneless skinless chicken breasts, diced
     3 cups sliced fresh mushrooms
     1 cup thinly sliced carrots
     1 cup frozen green peas, thawed and well drained
    ½ cup sliced spring onions
     1 teaspoon ground thyme
    ½ cup all-purpose flour
    3½ cups skim milk
    ½ cup dry sherry
    ½ teaspoon salt
    ¼ teaspoon ground red pepper
     1 (15-ounce) carton low-fat ricotta cheese
    1½ cups grated part-skim mozzarella cheese, divided
    ½ cup grated reduced-fat Swiss cheese

Prepare pasta according to package directions. Spray Dutch oven or large skillet with cooking spray; place over medium-high heat until hot. Add chicken and sauté 4 minutes or until cooked through. Drain well and remove chicken. Spray Dutch oven again with cooking spray and heat over medium-high heat until hot. Add mushrooms, carrots, peas, onions and thyme; sauté 6 minutes. Set aside.

Place flour in medium saucepan. Gradually add milk, stirring with wire whisk until blended; stir in sherry. Bring to a boil over medium heat and cook 5 minutes or until thickened, stirring constantly. Stir in salt and red pepper. Reserve one cup of sauce and set aside.

Combine ricotta cheese, 1 cup mozzarella cheese and Swiss cheese in large bowl.

Preheat oven to 350°F. Spread 1 cup of the sauce over bottom of 13×9×2-inch pan. Arrange 4 pieces of lasagne (3 lengthwise, 1 widthwise) over sauce. Top with half of ricotta cheese mixture, half of chicken mixture and half of remaining sauce mixture. Repeat layers, ending with 4 pieces of lasagne. Spread reserved 1 cup of sauce over last complete layer of lasagne, being sure to cover lasagne completely.

Cover lasagne with foil and bake 1 hour. Uncover, sprinkle remaining ½ cup mozzarella cheese over top. Bake, uncovered, 5 minutes. Cover; let stand 15 minutes before serving.   *Makes 10 servings*

Favorite recipe from **National Pasta Association**

Vegetable Lasagna

Tomato-Basil Sauce (recipe follows)
2 tablespoons olive oil
4 medium carrots, peeled, sliced diagonally
3 medium zucchini, thinly sliced
6 ounces spinach leaves, washed, stemmed and torn into bite-sized pieces
¼ teaspoon salt
¼ teaspoon black pepper
1 egg
3 cups ricotta cheese
½ cup plus 2 tablespoons grated Parmesan cheese, divided
12 uncooked lasagna noodles
1½ cups (6 ounces) shredded mozzarella cheese
1½ cups (6 ounces) shredded Monterey Jack cheese
Belgian endive leaves, Bibb lettuce leaves and fresh basil sprigs for garnish

1. Prepare Tomato-Basil Sauce.

2. Heat oil in large skillet over medium heat until hot. Add carrots; cook and stir 4 minutes. Add zucchini; cook and stir 8 minutes or until crisp-tender. Add spinach; cook and stir 1 minute or until spinach is wilted. Stir in salt and pepper. Remove from heat.

3. Preheat oven to 350°F. Beat egg in medium bowl. Stir in ricotta cheese and ½ cup Parmesan cheese.

4. Spread 1 cup Tomato-Basil Sauce in bottom of 13×9-inch baking pan; top with 4 uncooked lasagna noodles.

5. Spoon ⅓ of ricotta cheese mixture over noodles; carefully spread with spatula.

6. Spoon ⅓ of vegetable mixture over cheese. Top with 1 cup Tomato-Basil Sauce. Sprinkle with ½ cup each mozzarella and Monterey Jack cheeses. Repeat layers twice beginning with noodles and ending with mozzarella and Monterey Jack cheeses. Sprinkle with remaining 2 tablespoons Parmesan cheese. Carefully pour ½ cup water around sides of pan. Cover pan tightly with foil.

7. Bake lasagna 1 hour or until bubbly. Uncover; let stand 10 to 15 minutes. Cut into squares. Garnish, if desired. *Makes 8 servings*

Tomato-Basil Sauce

2 cans (28 ounces each) plum tomatoes
1 teaspoon olive oil
1 medium onion, chopped
3 cloves garlic, minced
1 tablespoon sugar
1 tablespoon dried basil leaves
¼ teaspoon salt
¼ teaspoon black pepper

1. Drain tomatoes, reserving ½ cup juice. Seed and chop tomatoes.

2. Heat oil in large skillet over medium heat until hot. Add onion and garlic; cook and stir 5 minutes or until tender. Stir in tomatoes, reserved juice, sugar, basil, salt and pepper.

3. Bring to a boil over high heat. Reduce heat to low. Simmer, uncovered, 25 to 30 minutes or until most of juices have evaporated.

Makes 4 cups

Vegetable Lasagna

Zesty Seafood Lasagna

2 packages (1.8 ounces each) white
    sauce mix
4½ cups milk
1 teaspoon dried basil leaves
½ teaspoon dried thyme leaves
½ teaspoon garlic powder
¾ cup grated Parmesan cheese, divided
3 tablespoons FRANK'S® Original
    REDHOT® Cayenne Pepper Sauce
9 oven-ready lasagna pasta sheets
2 packages (10 ounces each) frozen chopped
    spinach, thawed and squeezed
½ pound cooked shrimp
½ pound raw bay scallops or flaked imitation
    crabmeat
2 cups (8 ounces) shredded mozzarella
    cheese, divided

1. Preheat oven to 400°F. Prepare white sauce according to package directions using milk, basil, thyme and garlic powder in saucepan. Stir in ½ *cup* Parmesan and RedHot® sauce.

2. Spread *1 cup* sauce in bottom of greased 13×9×2-inch casserole. Layer 3 pasta sheets crosswise over sauce. (Do not let edges touch.) Layer *half* of the spinach and seafood over pasta. Spoon *1 cup* sauce over seafood; sprinkle with ¾ *cup* mozzarella. Repeat layers. Top with final layer of pasta, remaining sauce and cheeses.

3. Cover with greased foil; bake 40 minutes. Remove foil; bake 10 minutes or until top is browned and pasta is cooked. Let stand 15 minutes. *Makes 8 servings*

Rigatoni Vegetable Casserole

8 ounces Rigatoni, Ziti or other medium
    pasta shape, uncooked
3 carrots, thinly sliced diagonally
3 cups broccoli florets
3 tablespoons margarine
2 tablespoons minced onion
3 tablespoons all-purpose flour
2¼ cups skim milk
½ cup grated Edam cheese
    Salt and freshly ground black pepper

Lightly spray 2-quart casserole with nonstick cooking spray; set aside.

Prepare pasta according to package directions. Five minutes before pasta is done, add carrots to pasta; cook 3 minutes. Add broccoli to pasta; cook remaining 2 minutes. When pasta and vegetables are done, drain well.

Preheat oven to 375°F. Melt margarine in medium saucepan over low heat. Add onion and sauté about 2 minutes. Stir in flour and continue cooking and stirring until mixture thickens. Add milk and cheese and cook until cheese is melted. Season with salt and pepper to taste. Transfer pasta and vegetables to large bowl; add cheese sauce. Toss well. Transfer to prepared casserole. Bake 25 to 30 minutes or until heated through.
Makes 4 servings

Favorite recipe from **National Pasta Association**

Zesty Seafood Lasagna

Triple Pepper Tomato Provolone Lasagna

1 red bell pepper, chopped
1 yellow bell pepper, chopped
1 green bell pepper, chopped
1 package (8 ounces) sliced fresh
    mushrooms
½ cup chopped onion
1 cup thinly sliced zucchini
4 cloves garlic, minced
1½ cups vegetable juice cocktail
1 can (16 ounces) diced tomatoes, undrained
1½ to 1¾ teaspoons Italian seasoning
1 tablespoon olive oil
9 uncooked lasagna noodles
1 cup nonfat cottage cheese
⅓ cup grated Parmesan cheese, divided
4 ounces sliced reduced-fat provolone cheese

1. Preheat oven to 350°F. Combine peppers, mushrooms, onion, zucchini, garlic, vegetable juice cocktail, tomatoes and Italian seasoning in Dutch oven or large saucepan. Bring to a boil over high heat. Reduce heat to low; simmer, uncovered, 15 minutes. Remove from heat; stir in oil.

2. Spray 12×8-inch baking pan with nonstick cooking spray. Place 3 lasagna noodles on bottom of pan. Spread ⅓ of the sauce over noodles. Spread ½ cup cottage cheese evenly over sauce; sprinkle with 2 tablespoons Parmesan cheese. Repeat layers, ending with sauce.

3. Bake, uncovered, 1 hour or until bubbly. Tear provolone cheese into small pieces; place on top of lasagna. Sprinkle with remaining Parmesan cheese. Bake 5 minutes longer or until cheese is melted. Let stand 15 minutes before serving.

Makes 6 servings

Classic Macaroni and Cheese

2 cups elbow macaroni
3 tablespoons butter or margarine
¼ cup chopped onion (optional)
2 tablespoons all-purpose flour
½ teaspoon salt
⅛ teaspoon pepper
2 cups milk
2 cups (8 ounces) SARGENTO® Classic
    Supreme® or Fancy Supreme® Shredded
    Mild Cheddar Cheese, divided

Cook macaroni according to package directions; drain. In medium saucepan, melt butter and cook onion about 5 minutes or until tender. Stir in flour, salt and pepper. Gradually add milk and cook, stirring occasionally, until thickened. Remove from heat.

Add 1½ cups Cheddar cheese and stir until cheese melts.

Combine cheese sauce with cooked macaroni. Place in 1½-quart casserole; top with remaining ½ cup Cheddar cheese. Bake at 350°F 30 minutes or until bubbly and cheese is golden brown.

Makes 6 servings

Triple Pepper Tomato Provolone Lasagna

Artichoke-Olive Chicken Bake

1½ cups uncooked rotini pasta
1 tablespoon olive oil
1 medium onion, chopped
½ green bell pepper, chopped
2 cups shredded cooked chicken
1 can (14½ ounces) diced tomatoes with
   Italian-style herbs, undrained
1 can (14 ounces) artichoke hearts, drained
   and quartered
1 can (6 ounces) sliced black olives, drained
1 teaspoon dried Italian seasoning
2 cups (8 ounces) shredded mozzarella
   cheese
   Fresh basil sprig (for garnish)

Preheat oven to 350°F. Spray 13×9-inch baking dish with nonstick cooking spray.

Cook pasta according to package directions. Drain; set aside.

Meanwhile, heat oil in large deep skillet over medium heat until hot. Add onion and pepper; cook and stir 1 minute. Add chicken, tomatoes with juice, pasta, artichokes, olives and Italian seasoning; mix until combined.

Place half of chicken mixture in prepared dish; sprinkle with half of cheese. Top with remaining chicken mixture and cheese.

Bake, covered, 35 minutes or until hot and bubbly. Garnish with basil, if desired.

Makes 8 servings

Stuffed Shells Florentine

18 jumbo pasta shells
1 package (10 ounces) frozen chopped
   spinach, thawed and drained
1⅓ cups (2.8-ounce can) FRENCH'S®
   French Fried Onions, divided
2 eggs, beaten
¾ cup (4 ounces) chopped boiled ham
½ cup ricotta cheese
½ teaspoon Italian seasoning
½ teaspoon garlic powder
1 can (10¾ ounces) condensed cream of
   chicken soup
1 cup milk
½ cup grated Parmesan cheese

Preheat oven to 350°F. Cook pasta according to package directions using shortest cooking time. Drain; cool in single layer.

Combine spinach, ⅔ *cup* French Fried Onions, eggs, ham, ricotta cheese, Italian seasoning and garlic powder in large bowl; mix well. Spoon about 2 tablespoons mixture into each shell.

Combine soup, milk and Parmesan cheese in medium bowl. Pour half of the soup mixture into bottom of 2-quart shallow baking dish. Arrange shells in dish. Pour remaining soup mixture over shells.

Bake, uncovered, 30 minutes or until hot and bubbly. Sprinkle with remaining ⅔ *cup* onions. Bake 5 minutes or until onions are golden.

Makes 6 servings

Prep Time: 20 minutes
Cook Time: 45 minutes

Artichoke-Olive Chicken Bake

Hearty Manicotti

1¾ cups (15-ounce container) ricotta cheese
1 package (10 ounces) frozen chopped
    spinach, thawed, squeezed dry
½ cup (2 ounces) grated Parmesan cheese
1 egg
⅛ teaspoon ground black pepper
8 to 10 dry manicotti shells, cooked, drained
1⅓ cups (two 6-ounce cans) CONTADINA®
    Dalla Casa Buitoni Italian Paste with
    Roasted Garlic
1⅓ cups water
½ cup (2 ounces) shredded mozzarella cheese

COMBINE ricotta cheese, spinach, Parmesan
cheese, egg and pepper in medium bowl. Spoon
mixture into manicotti shells. Place in 12×7-inch
baking dish.

STIR together tomato paste and water in
medium bowl; pour over manicotti. Sprinkle with
mozzarella cheese.

BAKE, uncovered, in preheated 350°F oven
30 to 40 minutes or until heated through.

Makes 4 to 5 servings

Pasta Primavera Casserole

8 ounces uncooked rotini pasta
1 jar (12 ounces) chicken gravy
½ cup milk
1⅓ cups (2.8-ounce can) FRENCH'S®
    French Fried Onions, divided
1 small zucchini, thinly sliced
1 tomato, chopped
1 cup frozen peas, thawed and drained
1 cup (4 ounces) shredded mozzarella cheese
½ cup grated Parmesan cheese
2 tablespoons minced fresh basil *or*
    1 teaspoon dried basil leaves

Preheat oven to 350°F. Grease 2-quart oblong
baking dish. Cook pasta according to package
directions using shortest cooking time. Drain.
Return pasta to saucepan.

Add gravy, milk, ⅔ *cup* French Fried Onions,
zucchini, tomato, peas, cheeses and basil to pasta;
toss lightly. Spoon into prepared baking dish.

Bake, uncovered, 35 minutes or until heated
through, stirring halfway through cooking time.
Top with remaining ⅔ *cup* onions. Bake,
uncovered, 5 minutes or until onions are golden.

Makes 6 servings

Prep Time: 15 minutes
Cook Time: 40 minutes

Hearty Manicotti

Spicy Manicotti

3 cups ricotta cheese
1 cup grated Parmesan cheese, divided
2 eggs, lightly beaten
2½ tablespoons chopped fresh parsley
1 teaspoon dried Italian seasoning
½ teaspoon garlic powder
½ teaspoon salt
½ teaspoon black pepper
1 pound spicy Italian sausage, casings removed
1 can (28 ounces) crushed tomatoes in purée, undrained
1 jar (26 ounces) marinara or spaghetti sauce
8 ounces uncooked manicotti shells

Preheat oven to 375°F. Spray 13×9-inch baking dish with nonstick cooking spray.

Combine ricotta cheese, ¾ cup Parmesan cheese, eggs, parsley, Italian seasoning, garlic powder, salt and pepper in medium bowl; set aside.

Crumble sausage into large skillet; brown over medium-high heat until no longer pink, stirring to separate. Drain sausage on paper towels; drain fat from skillet.

Add tomatoes with juice and marinara sauce to same skillet; bring to a boil over high heat. Reduce heat to low; simmer, uncovered, 10 minutes. Pour about one third of sauce into prepared dish.

Stuff each uncooked shell with about ½ cup cheese mixture. Place in prepared dish. Top shells with sausage; pour remaining sauce over shells.

Cover tightly with foil and bake 50 minutes to 1 hour or until noodles are tender. Let stand 5 minutes before serving. Serve with remaining ¼ cup Parmesan cheese.   *Makes 8 servings*

Baked Provençal Ziti Provolone

10 ounces uncooked ziti
1 cup evaporated skimmed milk
½ cup skim milk
4 egg whites
1 tablespoon Dijon mustard
½ teaspoon salt
½ cup finely chopped green onions, with tops
4 ounces sliced provolone cheese
2 tablespoons grated Parmesan cheese
  Chives and red pepper for garnish

1. Preheat oven to 325°F. Spray 9-inch square baking pan with nonstick cooking spray; set aside. Cook pasta according to package directions, omitting salt; drain. Place in bottom of prepared pan; set aside.

2. Meanwhile, combine evaporated milk, skim milk, egg whites, mustard and salt in food processor or blender; process until smooth.

3. Sprinkle green onions over pasta. Pour egg mixture over top. Sprinkle with black pepper to taste and top with provolone cheese.

4. Bake 35 minutes or until heated through. Remove from oven. Sprinkle with Parmesan cheese. Let stand 5 minutes before serving. Garnish, if desired.   *Makes 4 servings*

Spicy Manicotti

Chili Spaghetti Casserole

8 ounces uncooked spaghetti
1 pound lean ground beef
1 medium onion, chopped
¼ teaspoon salt
⅛ teaspoon black pepper
1 can (15 ounces) vegetarian chili with
    beans
1 can (14½ ounces) Italian-style stewed
    tomatoes, undrained
1½ cups (6 ounces) shredded sharp Cheddar
    cheese, divided
½ cup reduced-fat sour cream
1½ teaspoons chili powder
¼ teaspoon garlic powder

Preheat oven to 350°F. Spray 13×9-inch baking dish with nonstick cooking spray.

Cook pasta according to package directions. Drain and place in prepared dish.

Meanwhile, place beef and onion in large skillet; sprinkle with salt and pepper. Brown beef over medium-high heat until beef is no longer pink, stirring to separate. Drain fat. Stir in chili, tomatoes with juice, 1 cup cheese, sour cream, chili powder and garlic powder.

Add chili mixture to pasta; stir until pasta is well coated. Sprinkle with remaining ½ cup cheese.

Cover tightly with foil and bake 30 minutes or until hot and bubbly. Let stand 5 minutes before serving.   *Makes 8 servings*

Manicotti Parmigiana

1 can (32 ounces) tomatoes, chopped
1 can (8 ounces) tomato sauce
1 package (1.5 ounces) LAWRY'S® Original
    Spaghetti Sauce Spices & Seasonings
2 tablespoons LAWRY'S® Garlic Spread
    Concentrate
1½ teaspoons LAWRY'S® Seasoned Salt
1 pound ground beef or turkey
¼ cup chopped green bell pepper
½ pound (about 2 cups) shredded mozzarella
    cheese
8 manicotti shells, cooked and drained
    Grated Parmesan cheese
    Finely chopped parsley for garnish

In large saucepan, combine tomatoes, tomato sauce, Spaghetti Sauce Spices & Seasonings, Garlic Spread Concentrate and Seasoned Salt; mix well. Bring to a boil over medium high heat. Reduce heat to low; simmer, covered, 20 minutes, stirring occasionally.

In medium skillet, brown ground beef and bell pepper until beef is crumbly; drain fat. Remove from heat; stir in mozzarella cheese. Stuff manicotti shells with beef mixture. Pour ¾ of spaghetti sauce in bottom of 12×8×2-inch baking dish. Place stuffed manicotti shells on sauce; top with remaining sauce. Sprinkle with Parmesan cheese. Bake, uncovered, in 375°F oven 30 minutes. Garnish with chopped parsley.
Makes 4 to 8 servings

Presentation: This recipe is easily doubled for a party.

Chili Spaghetti Casserole

Wisconsin Swiss Linguine Tart

½ cup butter, divided
2 cloves garlic, minced
30 thin French bread slices
3 tablespoons all-purpose flour
1 teaspoon salt
¼ teaspoon white pepper
    Dash ground nutmeg
2½ cups milk
¼ cup grated Wisconsin Parmesan cheese
2 eggs, beaten
8 ounces fresh linguine, cooked, drained
2 cups (8 ounces) shredded Wisconsin Swiss
    cheese, divided
⅓ cup sliced green onions
2 tablespoons minced fresh basil *or*
    1 teaspoon dried basil leaves
2 plum tomatoes, each cut lengthwise into
    eighths

Melt ¼ cup butter in small saucepan over medium heat. Add garlic; cook 1 minute. Brush 10-inch pie plate with half of the butter mixture. Line bottom and side of pie plate with bread, allowing up to 1-inch overhang. Brush bread with remaining butter mixture. Bake in preheated 400°F oven 5 minutes or until lightly browned. *Reduce oven temperature to 350°F.*

Melt remaining ¼ cup butter in medium saucepan over low heat. Stir in flour and seasonings. Gradually stir in milk; cook, stirring constantly, until thickened. Stir in Parmesan cheese. Stir some of the sauce into eggs; stir egg mixture into sauce. Set aside.

Combine linguine, 1¼ cups Swiss cheese, green onions and basil in large bowl. Pour sauce over linguine mixture; toss to coat. Pour into crust. Arrange tomatoes on top; sprinkle with remaining ¾ cup Swiss cheese.

Bake in preheated 350°F oven 25 minutes or until warm; let stand 5 minutes. Garnish as desired.   *Makes 8 servings*

Favorite recipe from **Wisconsin Milk Marketing Board**

Wisconsin Swiss Linguine Tart

Baked Chicken and Garlic Orzo

4 chicken breast halves, skinned
¼ cup dry white wine
10 ounces uncooked orzo pasta
1 cup chopped onions
4 cloves garlic, minced
2 tablespoons chopped fresh parsley
1 teaspoon dried oregano
1 can (about 14 ounces) fat-free reduced-
  sodium chicken broth
  Paprika
1 teaspoon lemon pepper
¼ teaspoon salt
2 teaspoons olive oil
1 lemon, cut into 8 wedges

1. Preheat oven to 350°F. Spray large nonstick skillet with cooking spray; heat over high heat until hot. Add chicken breast halves. Cook meat side down, 1 to 2 minutes or until lightly browned; set aside.

2. Reduce heat to medium-high; add wine. Stir with flat spatula, scraping brown bits from bottom of pan. Cook 30 seconds or until slightly reduced; set aside.

3. Spray 9-inch square baking pan with nonstick cooking spray. Add pasta, onions, garlic, parsley, oregano, chicken broth, ¼ cup water and wine mixture; stir. Place chicken breasts on top. Sprinkle lightly with paprika and lemon pepper. Bake, uncovered, 1 hour and 10 minutes. Remove chicken. Add salt and olive oil to baking pan; mix well. Place chicken on top. Serve with fresh lemon wedges. *Makes 4 servings*

Pastitso

8 ounces uncooked elbow macaroni
½ cup cholesterol-free egg substitute
¼ teaspoon ground nutmeg
¾ pound lean ground lamb, beef or turkey
½ cup chopped onion
1 clove garlic, minced
1 can (8 ounces) tomato sauce
¾ teaspoon dried mint leaves
½ teaspoon dried oregano
½ teaspoon black pepper
⅛ teaspoon ground cinnamon
2 teaspoons reduced-calorie margarine
3 tablespoons all-purpose flour
1½ cups skim milk
2 tablespoons grated Parmesan cheese

Cook pasta according to package directions. Drain and transfer to medium bowl; stir in egg substitute and nutmeg. Spray bottom of 9-inch square baking dish with nonstick cooking spray. Spread pasta mixture in baking dish. Set aside.

Preheat oven to 350°F. Cook lamb, onion and garlic in large nonstick skillet over medium heat until lamb is no longer pink. Stir in tomato sauce, mint, oregano, pepper and cinnamon. Reduce heat to low and simmer 10 minutes; spread over pasta.

Melt margarine in small saucepan over medium heat. Add flour. Stir 1 minute. Whisk in milk. Cook, stirring constantly, until thickened, about 6 minutes; spread over meat mixture. Sprinkle with cheese. Bake 30 to 40 minutes or until set.
Makes 6 servings

Baked Chicken and Garlic Orzo

Reuben Noodle Bake

    8 ounces uncooked egg noodles
    5 ounces thinly sliced corned beef
    1 can (14½ ounces) sauerkraut with
        caraway seeds, drained
    2 cups (8 ounces) shredded Swiss cheese
    ½ cup Thousand Island dressing
    ½ cup milk
    1 tablespoon prepared mustard
    2 slices pumpernickel bread
    1 tablespoon margarine or butter, melted
        Red onion slices

Preheat oven to 350°F. Spray 13×9-inch baking dish with nonstick cooking spray.

Cook noodles according to package directions. Drain; set aside.

Meanwhile, cut corned beef into bite-sized pieces. Combine noodles, corned beef, sauerkraut and cheese in large bowl. Pour into prepared dish.

Combine dressing, milk and mustard in small bowl. Spoon dressing mixture evenly over noodle mixture.

Tear bread into large pieces. Process in food processor or blender until crumbs are formed. Combine bread crumbs and margarine in small bowl; sprinkle evenly over casserole.

Bake, uncovered, 25 to 30 minutes or until heated through. Garnish with red onion, if desired.   *Makes 6 servings*

Baked Ditalini with Three Cheeses

    1 pound Ditalini, Elbow Macaroni or other
        medium pasta shape, uncooked
    1 cup skim milk
    ¾ cup part-skim ricotta cheese
    ½ cup shredded low-fat Cheddar cheese
    ⅓ cup plus 2 tablespoons grated Parmesan
        cheese, divided
    ¼ cup chopped fresh parsley
        Salt and freshly ground black pepper
    ¼ cup fine dry bread crumbs
    2 tablespoons melted margarine

Prepare pasta according to package directions, reducing cooking time by one third; drain.

Preheat oven to 375°F. While pasta is cooking, combine milk and ricotta cheese in blender; blend until smooth. Transfer to medium bowl; stir in Cheddar cheese, ⅓ cup Parmesan cheese, parsley, salt and pepper to taste.

Stir pasta into cheese mixture until well blended. Transfer to 10-inch round casserole. Stir bread crumbs, margarine and remaining 2 tablespoons of Parmesan cheese in small bowl until thoroughly mixed. Sprinkle mixture evenly over casserole.

Bake about 35 minutes or until heated through, bubbly around edges and bread crumbs are golden brown. Serve immediately.

Makes 6 side-dish servings

Favorite recipe from **National Pasta Association**

Reuben Noodle Bake

Shrimp in Angel Hair Pasta Casserole

1 tablespoon butter
1 cup half-and-half
1 cup plain yogurt
2 eggs
½ cup (4 ounces) shredded Swiss cheese
⅓ cup crumbled feta cheese
⅓ cup chopped fresh parsley
¼ cup chopped fresh basil *or* 1 teaspoon dried basil leaves
1 teaspoon dried oregano leaves
1 package (9 ounces) uncooked fresh angel hair pasta, divided
1 jar (16 ounces) thick and chunky salsa
1 pound raw medium shrimp, peeled and deveined, divided
½ cup (4 ounces) shredded Monterey Jack cheese
Snow peas (optional, for garnish)
Plum tomatoes stuffed with cottage cheese (optional, for garnish)

Preheat oven to 350°F. Grease 12×8-inch baking pan with butter. Combine half-and-half, yogurt, eggs, Swiss cheese, feta cheese, parsley, basil and oregano in bowl; mix well.

Spread half of the pasta on bottom of prepared pan. Cover with salsa. Add half of the shrimp. Cover with remaining pasta. Spread egg mixture over pasta and top with remaining shrimp. Sprinkle Monterey Jack cheese over top. Bake 30 minutes or until bubbly. Let stand 10 minutes. Garnish, if desired. *Makes 6 servings*

Favorite recipe from **Southeast United Dairy Industry Association, Inc.**

Sausage & Noodle Casserole

1 pound **BOB EVANS FARMS®** Original Recipe Roll Sausage
1 cup chopped onion
¼ cup chopped green bell pepper
1 (10-ounce) package frozen peas
1 (10¾-ounce) can condensed cream of chicken soup
1 (8-ounce) package egg noodles, cooked according to package directions and drained
Salt and black pepper to taste
1 (2.8-ounce) can French fried onions, crushed

Preheat oven to 350°F. Crumble sausage into large skillet. Add onion and green pepper. Cook over medium heat until meat is browned and vegetables are tender, stirring occasionally. Drain off any drippings. Cook peas according to package directions. Drain, reserving liquid in 2-cup glass measuring cup; set aside. Add enough water to pea liquid to obtain 1⅓ cups liquid. Combine liquid and soup in large bowl; stir in sausage mixture, noodles, reserved peas, salt and black pepper. Mix well. Spoon mixture into greased 2½-quart baking dish. Sprinkle with fried onions. Bake 30 minutes or until bubbly. Serve hot. Refrigerate leftovers. *Makes 6 servings*

Shrimp in Angel Hair Pasta Casserole

Mexican Chicken Casserole

8 ounces uncooked elbow macaroni or small shell pasta
2 teaspoons olive oil
1 large carrot, grated
1 medium green bell pepper, chopped
1 clove garlic, minced
¾ pound chicken tenders, cut into ¾-inch pieces
2 teaspoons ground cumin
1½ teaspoons dried oregano
½ teaspoon salt
¼ teaspoon ground red pepper
8 ounces (2 cups) shredded Monterey Jack cheese, divided
1 bottle (16 ounces) salsa, divided

1. Cook pasta according to package directions.

2. Meanwhile, heat oil in large nonstick skillet over medium heat. Add carrot, bell pepper and garlic; cook and stir 3 minutes or until vegetables are tender. Add chicken. Increase heat to medium-high; cook and stir 3 to 4 minutes or until chicken is no longer pink in center. Add cumin, oregano, salt and ground red pepper; cook and stir 1 minute. Remove from heat; set aside.

3. Grease 13×9-inch microwavable dish. Drain and rinse pasta under cold running water; place in large bowl. Add chicken mixture, 1 cup cheese and 1 cup salsa. Mix well; pour into prepared dish. Top with remaining 1 cup salsa and 1 cup cheese.

4. Cover with plastic wrap; microwave on HIGH (100%) 4 to 6 minutes, turning dish halfway through cooking time. Serve immediately.
Makes 4 to 6 servings

Baked Rigatoni with Sausage

½ pound Italian sausage, crumbled
2 cups low-fat milk
2 tablespoons all-purpose flour
½ pound rigatoni pasta, cooked and drained
2½ cups (10 ounces) shredded mozzarella cheese
¼ cup grated Parmesan cheese
1 teaspoon LAWRY'S® Garlic Salt
¾ teaspoon LAWRY'S® Seasoned Pepper
2 to 3 tablespoons dry bread crumbs *or*
¾ cup croutons

In large skillet, brown sausage 5 minutes; drain fat. Add milk and flour; mix well. Bring to a boil over medium high heat, stirring constantly. Remove from heat. Stir in pasta, cheeses, Garlic Salt and Seasoned Pepper.

Bake pasta mixture, uncovered, in ½-quart baking dish in 350°F oven 25 minutes. Sprinkle with bread crumbs; place under broiler to just brown.
Makes 6 servings

Serving Suggestion: Top with chopped parsley for garnish.

Hint: ¼ pound cooked diced ham can replace sausage.

Mexican Chicken Casserole

Tuna Noodle Casserole

1 can (10¾ ounces) condensed cream of
    mushroom soup
1 cup milk
3 cups hot cooked rotini pasta
    (2 cups uncooked)
1 can (12.5 ounces) tuna packed in water,
    drained and flaked
1⅓ cups (2.8-ounce can) FRENCH'S® French
    Fried Onions, divided
1 package (10 ounces) frozen peas and
    carrots
½ cup (2 ounces) shredded Cheddar or
    grated Parmesan cheese

Combine soup and milk in 2-quart microwavable
shallow casserole. Stir in pasta, tuna, ⅔ cup
French Fried Onions, vegetables and cheese.
Cover; microwave on HIGH (100%) 10 minutes
or until heated through, stirring halfway through
cooking time.* Top with remaining ⅔ cup onions.
Microwave 1 minute or until onions are golden.

Makes 6 servings

*Or, bake, covered, in 350°F oven 25 to 30 minutes.

Prep Time: 10 minutes
Cook Time: 11 minutes

Spinach Ziti Casserole

1 pound ziti or other pasta
2 teaspoons vegetable oil
1 medium onion, chopped
1 (16-ounce) can tomato sauce
1 (10-ounce) package frozen spinach,
    thawed and squeezed dry
2 tablespoons dried oregano leaves
2 teaspoons sugar
½ teaspoon black pepper
½ teaspoon chili powder
1 (16-ounce) container non-fat cottage
    cheese
1 (15-ounce) can kidney beans, drained and
    rinsed

Cook pasta according to package directions in
large saucepan. Drain and return to saucepan.

Meanwhile, heat oil in medium saucepan over
low heat. Add onion; cook and stir 5 minutes.
Stir in tomato sauce, spinach, oregano, sugar,
pepper and chili powder. Cook over low heat 15
minutes. Add sauce, cottage cheese and kidney
beans to pasta; mix together.

Pour into 2-quart baking dish; cover. Bake in
350°F oven 20 minutes.   *Makes 6 servings*

Note: If desired, recipe can be heated on the
stovetop. Do not remove pasta mixture from
saucepan. Heat thoroughly over medium heat,
stirring occasionally.

Favorite recipe from **The Sugar Association**

Tuna Noodle Casserole

Spinach-Cheese Pasta Casserole

8 ounces uncooked pasta shells
2 eggs
1 cup ricotta cheese
1 jar (26 ounces) marinara sauce
1 teaspoon salt
1 package (10 ounces) frozen chopped
    spinach, thawed and squeezed dry
1 cup (4 ounces) shredded mozzarella cheese
¼ cup grated Parmesan cheese

Preheat oven to 350°F. Spray 1½-quart round casserole with nonstick cooking spray.

Cook pasta according to package directions. Drain; set aside.

Meanwhile, whisk eggs in large bowl until blended. Add ricotta cheese; stir until combined.

Place pasta, marinara sauce and salt in large bowl; stir to coat pasta. Pour pasta mixture into prepared dish. Top with ricotta mixture and spinach. Sprinkle mozzarella and Parmesan cheeses evenly over casserole.

Bake, covered, 30 minutes. Uncover; bake 15 minutes or until hot and bubbly.

Makes 6 to 8 servings

Tortellini Bake Parmesano

1 package (12 ounces) fresh or frozen
    cheese tortellini or ravioli
½ pound lean ground beef
½ medium onion, finely chopped
2 cloves garlic, minced
½ teaspoon dried oregano, crushed
1 can (26 ounces) DEL MONTE® Chunky
    Spaghetti Sauce with Garlic & Herb
2 small zucchini, sliced
⅓ cup (about 1½ ounces) grated Parmesan
    cheese

1. Cook pasta according to package directions; rinse and drain.

2. Meanwhile, brown beef with onion, garlic and oregano in large skillet over medium-high heat; drain. Season with salt and pepper, if desired.

3. Add spaghetti sauce and zucchini. Cook 15 minutes or until thickened, stirring occasionally.

4. In oiled 2-quart microwavable dish, arrange half of pasta; top with half *each* of sauce and cheese. Repeat layers ending with cheese; cover.

5. Microwave on HIGH 8 to 10 minutes or until heated through, rotating dish halfway through cooking time.

Makes 4 servings

Prep & Cook Time: 35 minutes

Helpful Hint: For convenience, double recipe and freeze one for later use. The recipe can also be made ahead, refrigerated and heated just before serving (allow extra time in microwave if dish is chilled).

Spinach-Cheese Pasta Casserole

Magical

MINUTE MEALS

Spicy Tuna and Linguine with Garlic and Pine Nuts

2 tablespoons olive oil
4 cloves garlic, minced
2 cups sliced mushrooms
½ cup chopped onion
½ teaspoon crushed red pepper
2½ cups chopped plum tomatoes
1 can (14½ ounces) chicken broth *plus*
    water to equal 2 cups
½ teaspoon salt
¼ teaspoon coarsely ground black pepper
1 package (9 ounces) uncooked fresh
    linguine
1 can (12 ounces) STARKIST® Solid White
    Tuna, drained and chunked
⅓ cup chopped fresh cilantro
⅓ cup toasted pine nuts or almonds

In 12-inch skillet, heat olive oil over medium-high heat; sauté garlic, mushrooms, onion and red pepper until golden brown. Add tomatoes, chicken broth mixture, salt and black pepper; bring to a boil.

Separate uncooked linguine into strands; place in skillet and spoon sauce over. Reduce heat to simmer; cook, covered, 4 more minutes or until cooked through. Toss gently; add tuna and cilantro and toss again. Sprinkle with pine nuts.

Makes 4 to 6 servings

Prep Time: 12 minutes
Cook Time: 10 minutes

Spicy Tuna and Linguine with Garlic and Pine Nuts

Pasta with Spinach and Ricotta

8 ounces uncooked tri-colored rotini pasta
1 box (10 ounces) frozen chopped spinach,
    thawed and squeezed dry
2 teaspoons bottled minced garlic
1 cup fat-free or part-skim ricotta cheese
3 tablespoons grated Parmesan cheese,
    divided
    Salt and black pepper
    Fresh basil leaves for garnish (optional)

1. Cook pasta according to package directions; drain.

2. Meanwhile, coat large skillet with nonstick cooking spray; heat over medium-low heat. Add spinach and garlic; cook and stir 5 minutes. Stir in ricotta cheese, half of Parmesan cheese and ½ cup water; season with salt and pepper to taste.

3. Add pasta to skillet; toss to coat evenly. Sprinkle with remaining Parmesan cheese. Garnish with fresh basil leaves, if desired.

Makes 4 servings

Prep and Cook Time: 24 minutes

Note: For extra flavor and color, add chopped fresh tomato or canned diced tomatoes to skillet with pasta.

Tortellini with Three-Cheese Tuna Sauce

1 pound uncooked spinach or egg, cheese-
    filled tortellini
2 green onions, thinly sliced
1 clove garlic, minced
1 tablespoon butter or margarine
1 cup low-fat ricotta cheese
½ cup low-fat milk
1 can (9 ounces) STARKIST® Tuna,
    drained and broken into chunks
½ cup (2 ounces) shredded low-fat
    mozzarella cheese
¼ cup grated Parmesan or Romano cheese
2 tablespoons chopped fresh basil or
    2 teaspoons dried basil leaves, crushed
1 teaspoon grated lemon peel
    Fresh tomato wedges, red peppers and
    basil leaves for garnish (optional)

In large saucepan, cook tortellini in boiling salted water according to package directions. When tortellini are almost done, in separate large saucepan, cook and stir onions and garlic in butter 2 minutes. Whisk in ricotta cheese and milk. Add tuna, cheeses, basil and lemon peel. Cook over medium-low heat until mixture is heated through and cheeses are melted.

Drain pasta; add to sauce. Toss well to coat; garnish if desired. Serve immediately.

Makes 4 to 5 servings

Prep and Cook Time: 25 minutes

Pasta with Spinach and Ricotta

Celebration Pasta

2 cups fresh tortellini
1 bag (16 ounces) BIRDS EYE® frozen
    Farm Fresh Mixtures Broccoli, Corn
    & Red Peppers
1 tablespoon olive oil
1 teaspoon salt
1 teaspoon lemon juice
½ cup fresh or canned diced tomatoes

• In large saucepan, cook tortellini according to package directions; drain and return to saucepan.

• Cook vegetables according to package directions; drain and add to tortellini.

• In small bowl, combine oil, salt and lemon juice. Stir in tomatoes.

• Stir tomato mixture into pasta and vegetables; cook over medium heat 5 minutes or until heated through.   *Makes 4 servings*

Prep Time: 10 minutes
Cook Time: 10 minutes

Mostaccioli with Spinach and Feta

8 ounces mostaccioli or penne
2 tablespoons olive oil
3 cups chopped tomatoes
1 package (10 ounces) frozen chopped
    spinach, thawed, well drained
½ cup chopped green onions
1 package (8 ounces) ATHENOS® Feta
    Cheese with Basil & Tomato, crumbled

COOK pasta as directed on package; drain. Return to pan; toss with oil.

ADD tomatoes, spinach and onions; toss lightly. Cook and stir 2 minutes or until thoroughly heated.

ADD cheese; cook 1 minute.

Makes 8 servings

Prep Time: 10 minutes
Cook Time: 15 minutes

Fettuccine with Olive Pesto

10 ounces dried fettuccine
1½ cups whole pitted California ripe olives
3 tablespoons drained capers
4 teaspoons lemon juice
1 tablespoon olive oil
2 teaspoons Dijon mustard
2 to 3 cloves garlic, peeled
¼ cup finely chopped fresh basil
¼ cup grated Parmesan cheese

Cook fettuccine according to package directions. Meanwhile, combine olives, capers, lemon juice, oil, mustard and garlic in food processor or blender. Puree until coarse. Stir in chopped basil and cheese; set aside.

Drain pasta well; transfer to large warm serving bowl. Spoon pesto over pasta; mix gently. Garnish with basil sprigs.   *Makes 4 servings*

Prep Time: about 15 minutes
Cook Time: about 15 minutes

Favorite recipe from **California Olive Industry**

Celebration Pasta

Penne with Artichokes

1 package (10 ounces) frozen artichoke
    hearts, thawed
1¼ cups water
2 tablespoons lemon juice
5 cloves garlic
2 tablespoons olive oil, divided
2 ounces oil-packed sun-dried tomatoes,
    drained
2 small dried hot red chilies, crushed
2 tablespoons chopped fresh parsley
¼ teaspoon salt
¼ teaspoon black pepper
¾ cup fresh bread crumbs
1 tablespoon chopped garlic
12 ounces penne, cooked and drained
1 tablespoon grated Romano cheese

Cook artichoke hearts in water and lemon juice
in medium saucepan over medium heat until
tender. Remove artichoke hearts from cooking
liquid; reserve liquid. Cool artichoke hearts; cut
into quarters.

Cook and stir garlic in 1 tablespoon plus 1½
teaspoons oil in large skillet over medium-high
heat until golden. Reduce heat to low. Add
artichoke hearts and tomatoes; simmer 1 minute.
Stir in reserved artichoke cooking liquid, chilies,
parsley, salt and pepper. Simmer 5 minutes.
Remove and discard garlic cloves.

Meanwhile, cook and stir bread crumbs and
1 tablespoon chopped garlic in remaining 1½
teaspoons oil. Pour artichoke sauce over penne
in large bowl; toss gently to coat. Sprinkle with
bread crumb mixture and cheese.

Makes 4 to 6 servings

Favorite recipe from **National Pasta Assocation**

Sausage Bake

1 cup uncooked egg noodles
1 bag (16 ounces) BIRDS EYE® frozen Cut
    Green Beans
1 pound smoked sausage links, fully cooked
1 can (15 ounces) cream of celery soup
½ teaspoon *each* sage, celery salt and garlic
    powder

• In large saucepan, cook noodles according to
package directions. Add green beans during last
10 minutes; drain and return to pan.

• Meanwhile, cut sausage into ½-inch pieces.

• Add all ingredients to noodles and beans; toss
together. Cook over medium heat 3 to 5 minutes
or until heated through. Add salt and pepper to
taste.

Makes 4 servings

Prep Time: 2 minutes
Cook Time: 15 minutes

Penne with Artichokes

Tempting Tuna Parmesano

1 package (9 ounces) refrigerated fresh angel hair pasta
¼ cup butter or margarine
2 large cloves garlic, peeled and minced
1 cup whipping cream
1 cup frozen peas
¼ teaspoon salt
1 can (6½ ounces) white tuna in water, drained
¼ cup grated Parmesan cheese

1. Cook pasta according to package directions. (Do not overcook.) Drain; set aside.

2. Place butter and garlic in large skillet; cook over medium-high heat until butter is melted. Stir in cream, peas and salt; bring to a boil.

3. Break tuna into chunks and stir into skillet with ¼ cup cheese. Stir pasta into skillet; cook until heated through, tossing gently with 2 wooden spoons. Serve with additional cheese and black pepper to taste. *Makes 2 to 3 servings*

Prep and Cook Time: 16 minutes

Speedy Mac & Cheese

1 can (10¾ ounces) condensed Cheddar cheese soup
1 cup milk
4 cups hot cooked medium shell macaroni (3 cups uncooked)
1⅓ cups (2.8-ounce can) FRENCH'S® French Fried Onions, divided
1 cup (4 ounces) shredded Cheddar cheese

Combine soup and milk in 2-quart microwavable casserole. Stir in macaroni, ⅔ *cup* French Fried Onions and cheese. Cover; microwave on HIGH (100%) 10 minutes or until heated through, stirring after 5 minutes.* Top with remaining ⅔ *cup* onions. Microwave 1 minute or until onions are golden. *Makes 6 servings*

*Or, bake, covered, in 350°F oven 25 to 30 minutes.

Prep Time: 10 minutes
Cook Time: 11 minutes

Garlic Parmesan Pasta

½ cup butter
2 teaspoons dried basil leaves
2 teaspoons lemon juice
1¼ teaspoons LAWRY'S® Garlic Powder with Parsley
¾ teaspoon LAWRY'S® Seasoned Salt
8 ounces fettuccine noodles, cooked and drained
1½ cups broccoli flowerettes, cooked until crisp-tender
3 tablespoons chopped walnuts
½ cup (2 ounces) grated Parmesan or Romano cheese

In large skillet, melt butter over medium heat. Add basil, lemon juice, Garlic Powder with Parsley and Seasoned Salt; mix well. Add hot fettuccine, broccoli and walnuts; mix well until pasta is well coated and ingredients are heated through. Add cheese; toss lightly to coat.
Makes 4 servings

Tempting Tuna Parmesano

Pork Pasta Fazool

½ pound lean ground pork
1 small onion, diced
1 clove garlic, minced
1 can (15 ounces) cannellini (white kidney beans), drained
1 can (14½ ounces) chicken broth
1 can (14½ ounces) Italian-style chopped tomatoes
½ cup small pasta shells or macaroni
1 teaspoon dried oregano leaves
½ teaspoon salt
½ teaspoon crushed fennel seed
½ teaspoon coarsely ground black pepper
¼ teaspoon crushed red pepper flakes

In large heavy saucepan, brown and crumble ground pork. Stir in onion and garlic; cook and stir until onion is soft, about 3 minutes. Stir in all remaining ingredients; bring to a boil, reduce heat and simmer 10 to 12 minutes or until pasta is tender.   *Makes 6 (1-cup) servings*

Prep Time: 20 minutes

Favorite recipe from **National Pork Producers Council**

Linguine with Oil and Garlic

½ cup FILIPPO BERIO® Extra-Virgin Flavorful Olive Oil, divided
10 cloves garlic, minced
12 ounces uncooked linguine
¼ teaspoon pepper
¼ teaspoon salt (optional)

1. Heat 2 tablespoons olive oil in small saucepan over medium heat. Add garlic; cook and stir until lightly browned. Remove from heat; set aside.

2. Cook linguine according to package directions until tender. *(Do not overcook.)*

3. Drain linguine; return to pan. Add garlic mixture, remaining 6 tablespoons olive oil, pepper and salt; toss lightly to coat.   *Makes 4 servings*

Prep Time: 5 minutes
Cook Time: 20 minutes

Bistro Chicken with Feta

2 cups cooked penne or rotini pasta, drained
2 boneless skinless chicken breast halves, grilled or broiled, cut into ¼-inch slices
1 cup quartered cherry tomatoes
1 package (4 ounces) ATHENOS® Crumbled Feta Cheese with Basil & Tomato
½ cup prepared GOOD SEASONS® Honey Mustard or Gourmet Caesar Salad Dressing
⅓ cup lightly packed fresh basil leaves, cut into strips
¼ cup chopped red onion
¼ cup sun-dried tomatoes, drained, chopped

TOSS all ingredients in large serving bowl. Serve warm or chilled.   *Makes 4 servings*

Prep Time: 25 minutes

Italian Meat Loaf Patties

2 packages (12 ounces each) extra wide
  noodles
2 tablespoons butter or margarine, melted
1 can (15 ounces) DEL MONTE® Italian
  or Original Sloppy Joe Sauce
2 pounds ground beef or turkey
1 cup dry bread crumbs
2 eggs, beaten
1 tablespoon dried minced onion

1. Preheat oven to 375°F.

2. Cook noodles according to package directions;
drain. Toss with butter; keep hot.

3. Set aside half of sauce to brush on patties.
In large bowl, combine remaining sauce with
remaining ingredients; mix with fork. On large,
greased baking sheet, shape meat mixture into
8 (1-inch-thick) oblong patties. Brush reserved
sauce over patties.

4. Bake 20 minutes or until no longer pink in
center. Serve patties with hot, buttered noodles.
Garnish, if desired.   *Makes 8 servings*

Prep Time: 5 minutes
Cook Time: 20 minutes

Zucchini Meat Sauce with Pasta

1 package (12 ounces) shell macaroni or
  corkscrew pasta
2 pounds ground beef
2 onions, chopped
2 cans (26½ ounces each) DEL MONTE®
  Spaghetti Sauce—Garlic & Herb
1 can (14½ ounces) DEL MONTE®
  FreshCut™ Diced Tomatoes, undrained
2 small zucchini, thinly sliced

1. In 8-quart pot, cook pasta according to
package directions; drain. Keep pasta hot.

2. In 6-quart pot, brown meat over medium-high
heat. Season with salt and pepper, if desired;
drain. Add onions; cook until tender. Stir in
spaghetti sauce and tomatoes; cook 5 minutes,
stirring occasionally. (Pour half of sauce into
freezer container; cool, cover and freeze for
another meal.)

3. Add zucchini to remaining sauce; cover and
cook over medium heat 7 to 10 minutes or until
zucchini is tender. Serve sauce over hot pasta.
Sprinkle with grated Parmesan cheese and
garnish, if desired.   *Makes 4 servings*

Prep & Cook Time: 30 minutes

Pasta Waldorf

8 ounces uncooked small shell pasta
2 Red Delicious apples, unpeeled
1 rib celery
½ cup chopped pecans
½ cup raisins
⅓ cup nonfat lemon yogurt
⅓ cup reduced-calorie mayonnaise

1. Cook pasta according to package directions; drain. Rinse in cold water; drain again.

2. Meanwhile, core and dice apples. Chop celery.

3. Combine pasta, apples, celery, pecans, raisins, yogurt and mayonnaise in large bowl. Toss gently until blended. Season to taste with salt. Cover and chill 5 minutes.   *Makes 6 side-dish servings*

Prep, Cook and Chill Time: 20 minutes

Savory Cheese Tortellini

2 pounds VELVEETA® Pasteurized Process
    Cheese Spread, cubed
¼ cup milk
¼ teaspoon ground nutmeg
1 package (7 ounces) cheese-filled tortellini,
    cooked and drained

Combine process cheese spread, milk and nutmeg in medium saucepan. Stir over low heat until process cheese spread is melted. Add hot tortellini; mix lightly. Garnish as desired.
Makes 4 servings

Prep Time: 10 minutes
Cook Time: 10 minutes

Microwave: Combine process cheese spread, milk and nutmeg in 1-quart microwave-safe bowl. Microwave on HIGH (100%) 2½ to 4½ minutes or until process cheese spread is melted, stirring after 2 minutes. Add hot tortellini; mix lightly.

Shrimp & Asparagus Fettuccine

12 ounces uncooked fettuccine
1 box (10 ounces) BIRDS EYE® frozen
    Asparagus Cuts*
1 tablespoon vegetable oil
1 package (16 ounces) frozen, uncooked
    cocktail-size shrimp
1 jar (12 ounces) prepared alfredo sauce
1 jar (4 ounces) sliced pimiento, drained

*Or, substitute 1½ cups Birds Eye® frozen Green Peas or Birds Eye® frozen Broccoli Cuts.

• Cook pasta according to package directions, adding asparagus to water 8 minutes before pasta is done. Drain; keep warm.

• Heat oil in large skillet over medium-high heat. Add shrimp; cover and cook 3 minutes or until shrimp turn pink. Drain excess liquid, leaving shrimp and 2 tablespoons liquid in skillet. Reduce heat. Add alfredo sauce and pimiento. Cover; cook 5 minutes. Do not boil.

• Toss fettuccine and asparagus with shrimp.
Makes about 4 servings

Prep Time: 5 minutes
Cook Time: 20 minutes

Pasta Waldorf

Garden Primavera Pasta

6 ounces bow-tie pasta
1 jar (6 ounces) marinated artichoke hearts
2 cloves garlic, minced
½ teaspoon dried rosemary, crushed
1 green bell pepper, cut into thin strips
1 large carrot, cut into 3-inch julienne strips
1 medium zucchini, cut into 3-inch julienne strips
1 can (14½ ounces) DEL MONTE® Pasta Style Chunky Tomatoes
12 small pitted ripe olives (optional)

Cook pasta according to package directions; drain. Drain artichokes, reserving marinade. Toss pasta in 3 tablespoons artichoke marinade; set aside.

Cut artichoke hearts into halves. In large skillet, cook garlic and rosemary in 1 tablespoon artichoke marinade. Add bell pepper, carrot, zucchini, tomatoes and olives, if desired. Cook, uncovered, over medium-high heat 4 to 5 minutes or until vegetables are crisp-tender and sauce is thickened. Add artichoke hearts. Spoon over pasta. Serve with grated Parmesan cheese, if desired.

Makes 4 servings

Prep Time: 15 minutes
Cook Time: 10 minutes

Eggplant Pasta Bake

4 ounces bow-tie pasta
1 pound eggplant, diced
1 clove garlic, minced
¼ cup olive oil
1½ cups shredded Monterey Jack cheese, divided
1 cup sliced green onions
½ cup grated Parmesan cheese
1 can (14½ ounces) DEL MONTE® Pasta Style Chunky Tomatoes

Preheat oven to 350°F. Cook pasta according to package directions; drain. In large skillet, cook eggplant and garlic in oil over medium-high heat until tender. Toss eggplant with cooked pasta, 1 cup Jack cheese, green onions and Parmesan cheese. Place in greased 9-inch square baking dish. Top with tomatoes and remaining ½ cup Jack cheese. Bake 15 minutes or until heated through.

Makes 6 servings

Prep & Cook Time: 30 minutes

Garden Primavera Pasta

Broccoli and Beef Pasta

1 pound lean ground beef
2 cloves garlic, minced
1 can (14½ ounces) beef broth
1 medium onion, thinly sliced
1 cup uncooked rotini pasta
½ teaspoon dried basil leaves
½ teaspoon dried oregano leaves
½ teaspoon dried thyme leaves
1 can (14½ ounces) Italian-style tomatoes, undrained
2 cups broccoli florets *or* 1 package (10 ounces) frozen broccoli, thawed
3 ounces shredded Cheddar cheese or grated Parmesan cheese

1. Combine beef and garlic in large nonstick skillet; cook over high heat 6 to 8 minutes or until beef is no longer pink. Pour off drippings. Place beef mixture in large bowl; set aside.

2. Add broth, onion, pasta, basil, oregano and thyme to skillet; bring to a boil. Reduce heat to medium-high and boil 10 minutes; add tomatoes and juice. Increase heat to high and bring to a boil; stir in broccoli. Cook, uncovered, 6 to 8 minutes, stirring occasionally, until broccoli is crisp-tender and pasta is tender. Return beef to skillet and stir 3 to 4 minutes or until heated.

3. With slotted spoon, transfer pasta to serving platter. Sprinkle with cheese. Cover with lid or tent with foil several minutes until cheese melts. Meanwhile, bring juice left in skillet to a boil over high heat. Boil until thick and reduced to 3 to 4 tablespoons. Spoon over beef.

Makes 4 servings

Prep and Cook Time: 30 minutes

Hot Sesame Noodles

1 package (16 ounces) uncooked linguini
1 teaspoon Oriental sesame oil
3 tablespoons olive oil
3 tablespoons sesame seeds
2 cloves garlic, minced
⅔ cup chunky peanut butter
1 cup chicken broth
⅓ cup reduced-sodium soy sauce
3 to 4 tablespoons FRANK'S® Original REDHOT® Cayenne Pepper Sauce
1½ teaspoons sugar
1 large green onion, sliced

1. Cook linguini according to package directions. Rinse under cold water; drain well. Toss linguini with sesame oil in large bowl.

2. Heat olive oil in large nonstick skillet over medium heat. Add sesame seeds and garlic; cook and stir constantly 1 minute or until seeds are golden. Add peanut butter; stir until well blended. Stir in broth, soy sauce, RedHot® sauce and sugar. Bring just to a boil.

3. Pour sauce over linguini; toss to coat evenly. Sprinkle with green onion. Serve immediately.

Makes 4 servings (2 cups sauce)

Note: Sesame noodles may be served cold, if desired. Chill linguini and sauce separately. Toss just before serving.

Prep Time: 20 minutes
Cook Time: 15 minutes

Broccoli and Beef Pasta

Milano Shrimp Fettuccine

   4 ounces egg or spinach fettuccine
   ½ pound raw medium shrimp, peeled and deveined
   1 clove garlic, minced
   1 tablespoon olive oil
   1 can (14½ ounces) DEL MONTE® *FreshCut*™ Diced Tomatoes with Basil, Garlic & Oregano, undrained
   ½ cup whipping cream
   ¼ cup sliced green onions

1. Cook pasta according to package; drain.

2. Meanwhile, cook shrimp and garlic in hot oil in large skillet over medium-high heat until shrimp are pink and opaque.

3. Stir in tomatoes; simmer 5 minutes. Blend in cream and green onions; heat through. (*Do not boil.*) Serve over hot pasta.

Makes 3 to 4 servings

Prep & Cook Time: 20 minutes

All-in-One Burger Stew

   1 pound lean ground beef
   2 cups frozen Italian vegetables
   1 can (14½ ounces) chopped tomatoes with basil and garlic
   1 can (about 14 ounces) beef broth
   2½ cups uncooked medium egg noodles

1. Cook beef in Dutch oven or large skillet over medium-high heat until no longer pink, breaking meat apart with wooden spoon. Drain drippings.

2. Add vegetables, tomatoes and broth; bring to a boil over high heat.

3. Add noodles; reduce heat to medium. Cover and cook 12 to 15 minutes or until noodles have absorbed liquid and vegetables are tender. Add salt and pepper to taste. Garnish if desired.

Makes 6 servings

Prep and Cook Time: 25 minutes

Chicken and Pasta in Cream Sauce

   6 tablespoons unsalted butter
   1 tablespoon CHEF PAUL PRUDHOMME'S® Poultry Magic®
   ½ pound finely chopped boneless skinless chicken breasts
   ¼ cup finely chopped green onions with tops
   2 cups heavy cream or half-and-half
   5 ounces thin spaghetti, cooked and drained

In large skillet, melt butter over medium heat. Add Poultry Magic® and chicken; cook 1 minute. Add onions; cook and stir 1 to 2 minutes. Gradually add cream, stirring until well blended. Bring to a boil. Reduce heat to low; simmer 2 to 3 minutes, until sauce starts to thicken, stirring frequently. Add hot spaghetti; toss. Heat, stirring occasionally. Serve immediately.

Makes 2 main-dish servings

Milano Shrimp Fettuccine

Chicken and Tomatoes in Red Pepper Cream

9 ounces refrigerated angel hair pasta
1 jar (7 ounces) roasted red peppers, drained
⅓ cup half-and-half
2 teaspoons Dijon mustard
1 teaspoon salt
12 sun-dried tomatoes (packed in oil), drained
1 tablespoon olive oil
4 boneless skinless chicken breast halves
    (about 1 pound)
    Black pepper
    Grated Parmesan cheese

1. Cook pasta according to package directions; drain.

2. Meanwhile, combine red peppers, half-and-half, mustard and salt in food processor or blender; cover and process until smooth. Set aside.

3. Rinse tomatoes in warm water; drain and pat dry. Cut in half.

4. Heat olive oil in large skillet over medium-high heat until hot. Add chicken and tomatoes. Cook chicken, uncovered, 3 minutes on each side.

5. Add red pepper mixture. Simmer 3 minutes or until sauce thickens slightly and chicken is no longer pink in center. Season with freshly ground black pepper to taste.

6. Serve chicken and sauce over pasta. Sprinkle with Parmesan cheese.   *Makes 4 servings*

Prep and cook time: 15 minutes

Spaghetti with Puttanesca Sauce

1 box (8 ounces) spaghetti or linguine
1 box (9 ounces) BIRDS EYE® frozen
    Deluxe Italian Green Beans
1 jar (15 ounces) spaghetti sauce
½ cup sliced, pitted ripe olives
1 can (2 ounces) anchovies, drained and
    mashed
1 teaspoon crushed red pepper flakes

• In large saucepan, cook spaghetti according to package directions. Add beans during last 5 minutes; drain and keep warm.

• Meanwhile, in medium saucepan, combine spaghetti sauce, olives and anchovies. Bring to boil over high heat; reduce heat to medium and simmer 5 minutes. Season with pepper flakes.

• Serve over spaghetti and beans.

Makes 4 servings

Prep Time: 5 minutes

Cook Time: 15 minutes

Variation: Add 1 tablespoon drained capers to sauce with olives.

Chicken and Tomatoes in Red Pepper Cream

Asian Chicken and Noodles

1 package (3 ounces) chicken flavor instant ramen noodles
1 bag (16 ounces) BIRDS EYE® frozen Farm Fresh Mixtures Broccoli, Carrots and Water Chestnuts*
1 tablespoon vegetable oil
1 pound boneless skinless chicken breasts, cut into thin strips
¼ cup stir-fry sauce

*Or, substitute 1 bag (16 ounces) Birds Eye® frozen Broccoli Cuts.

• Reserve seasoning packet from noodles.

• Bring 2 cups water to boil in large saucepan. Add noodles and vegetables. Cook 3 minutes, stirring occasionally; drain.

• Meanwhile, heat oil in large nonstick skillet over medium-high heat. Add chicken; cook and stir until browned, about 8 minutes.

• Stir in noodles, vegetables, stir-fry sauce and reserved seasoning packet; heat through.

Makes about 4 servings

Prep Time: 5 minutes
Cook Time: 20 minutes

Pork with Vegetables and Linguine

1 pound boneless pork shoulder, cut into ¼×½×2-inch strips
1 medium onion, thinly sliced
2 tablespoons Worcestershire sauce
1 tablespoon reduced-sodium soy sauce
2 teaspoons cornstarch
½ teaspoon curry or chili powder
½ teaspoon kitchen browning sauce
½ pound broccoli, stems thinly sliced and separated from florets
2 cups hot, cooked and drained linguine or medium noodles
1 large tomato, cut into small pieces

Combine pork, onion, Worcestershire, soy sauce, cornstarch, curry powder and browning sauce in microwavable 2-quart casserole. Marinate 10 to 15 minutes at room temperature.

Cover casserole with waxed paper; microwave on HIGH (100%) 4 to 5 minutes, stirring at 2 minute intervals, until pork is no longer pink. Stir in broccoli stems; cover and microwave 1 minute. Stir in florets; noodles and tomato; microwave 1 minute or until heated through. Season to taste with salt and pepper.

Makes 4 servings

Prep Time: 10 minutes
Cook Time: 10 minutes

Favorite recipe from **National Pork Producers Council**

Asian Chicken and Noodles

Creamy Chicken Florentine

    8 ounces uncooked fusilli
    1 package (8 ounces) cream cheese
    ½ cup canned chicken broth
    ½ teaspoon dried Italian seasoning
    ¼ teaspoon salt
    ¼ teaspoon black pepper
      Dash hot pepper sauce
    1 box (10 ounces) frozen chopped spinach,
      thawed and squeezed dry
    1 can (10 ounces) premium chunk white
      chicken in water, drained
    1 tablespoon lemon juice

1. Cook pasta according to package directions; drain.

2. Combine cream cheese, broth, Italian seasoning, salt, black pepper and hot pepper sauce in microwavable 2-quart casserole. Cover and microwave at HIGH (100%) 2 to 3 minutes; whisk until smooth and blended.

3. Add spinach, chicken and lemon juice. Microwave at HIGH 2 to 3 minutes or until hot, stirring after 1 minute.

4. Combine pasta and spinach mixture in large bowl; toss until blended.   *Makes 4 servings*

Prep and cook time: 20 minutes

Pork, Pepper, Pasta and Peas

    4 ounces cooked lean pork loin, cut into
      julienne strips
    1½ cups medium macaroni, cooked and
      drained
    1 cup frozen peas, thawed
    1 small red bell pepper, seeded and chopped
    2 medium carrots, sliced diagonally
    3 tablespoons red wine vinegar
    2 tablespoons vegetable oil
    1 clove garlic, minced
    ½ teaspoon Italian seasoning
    ½ teaspoon sugar
    ½ teaspoon salt
    ½ teaspoon black pepper
    ½ cup (2 ounces) shredded mild Cheddar
      cheese

Combine pork, macaroni, peas and bell pepper in large serving bowl; set aside. Steam carrots in small microwavable bowl or steamer until crisp-tender; add to pork mixture.

For dressing, place remaining ingredients, except cheese, in jar with tight-fitting lid; shake well. Pour over pork mixture. Toss gently to coat. Sprinkle shredded cheese over mixture; toss gently. Serve immediately or refrigerate, covered, up to 24 hours.   *Makes 4 (1½-cup) servings*

Preparation Time: 15 minutes

Favorite recipe from **National Pork Producers Council**

Creamy Chicken Florentine

Cheesy Herb-Stuffed Mushrooms with Spinach Fettuccine

2 packages (9 ounces each) fresh spinach
    fettuccine
$\frac{1}{3}$ cup extra-virgin olive oil
1 tablespoon dried basil leaves
2 cloves garlic, minced
1 package ($6\frac{1}{2}$ ounces) garlic and herb soft
    spreadable cheese
16 large mushrooms, rinsed and stems
    removed

1. Prepare barbecue grill for direct cooking.

2. Cook fettuccine according to package directions. Drain; return to saucepan. Set aside.

3. Meanwhile, combine oil, basil and garlic in small bowl; pour over cooked pasta. Toss well; set aside.

4. Cut aluminum foil into 4 large squares. Spoon about 1 tablespoon cheese into each mushroom cap. Place four mushroom caps, cheese-sides-up, in center of each square. Fold aluminum foil over mushrooms to close, leaving small air pocket directly above cheese.

5. Place packets on grid. Grill, on covered grill, over hot coals 5 minutes or until mushroom caps are fork-tender. Remove from grill.

6. Transfer fettuccine to serving bowl. Remove mushroom caps from packets; arrange over fettuccine. Serve immediately.

Makes 4 to 6 servings

Prep and Cook Time: 30 minutes

Tomato Pesto Lasagna

8 ounces lasagna noodles (2 inches wide)
1 pound crumbled sausage or ground beef
1 can ($14\frac{1}{2}$ ounces) DEL MONTE®
    FreshCut™ Diced Tomatoes with Garlic
    & Onion, undrained
1 can (6 ounces) DEL MONTE® Tomato
    Paste
8 ounces ricotta cheese
1 package (4 ounces) pesto sauce*
2 cups (8 ounces) shredded mozzarella
    cheese

*Pesto sauce is available frozen or refrigerated at the supermarket.

1. Cook noodles according to package directions; rinse, drain and separate noodles.

2. Meanwhile, brown meat in large skillet; drain. Stir in tomatoes, tomato paste and $\frac{3}{4}$ cup water.

3. Layer $\frac{1}{3}$ meat sauce, then half each of noodles, ricotta cheese, pesto and mozzarella cheese in 2-quart casserole or 9-inch square baking dish; repeat layers. Top with remaining sauce. Sprinkle with grated Parmesan cheese, if desired.

4. Bake at 350°F 30 minutes or until heated through. *Makes 6 servings*

Prep Time: 20 minutes

Cook Time: 30 minutes

Microwave Directions: Assemble lasagna in 9-inch square microwavable dish as directed. Cover with vented plastic wrap; microwave on HIGH 10 minutes, rotating dish after 5 minutes.

Cheesy Herb-Stuffed Mushrooms with Spinach Fettuccine

Sun-Dried Tomato Pesto with Tortellini

2 packages (9 ounces each) refrigerated
    three-cheese tortellini
10 oil-packed sun-dried tomatoes
½ cup fresh parsley leaves, coarsely chopped
¼ cup fresh basil leaves, coarsely chopped
¼ cup (1 ounce) grated Parmesan cheese
¼ cup toasted slivered almonds or walnuts
3 cloves garlic
2 teaspoons olive oil
    Fresh basil leaves for garnish (optional)

1. Cook pasta according to package directions;
reserve cooking water.

2. Combine tomatoes, parsley, basil, Parmesan,
almonds, garlic and oil in food processor or
blender; process until well blended. (If pesto is
too dry, add hot pasta cooking water, 1 teaspoon
at a time, until desired consistency.)

3. Combine tortellini and pesto in serving bowl;
toss to coat evenly. Garnish with fresh basil
leaves, if desired.   *Makes 6 servings*

Prep and Cook Time: 20 minutes

Eggplant & Feta Ziti

1 pound ground beef
1 medium eggplant, peeled, cut into ½-inch
    cubes (about 6 cups)
½ cup chopped onion
1 clove garlic, minced
1 jar (32 ounces) spaghetti sauce
¼ teaspoon ground cinnamon
1 package (8 ounces) ATHENOS® Feta
    Cheese with Garlic & Herb, crumbled
2 cups (8 ounces) shredded low-moisture
    part-skim mozzarella cheese
2 cups ziti, cooked, drained

BROWN meat in large skillet; drain. Remove
and set aside. Cook eggplant, onion and garlic on
medium heat 10 minutes or until vegetables are
tender, stirring occasionally. Stir in spaghetti
sauce, cinnamon and reserved meat. Reduce heat
to low; simmer 5 minutes. Mix feta and mozzarella
cheese in small bowl.

LAYER ziti, meat sauce and cheese mixture in
greased 13×9-inch baking dish.

BAKE at 375°F for 25 to 30 minutes or until
thoroughly heated and lightly browned. Let stand
10 minutes before serving.

Makes 8 to 10 servings

Prep Time: 35 minutes
Baking Time: 30 minutes plus standing

Sun-Dried Tomato Pesto with Tortellini

Dynamic DINNER DISHES

Italian Garden Fusilli

1¾ cups (14.5-ounce can) CONTADINA®
    Dalla Casa Buitoni Recipe Ready Diced
    Tomatoes, undrained
1 cup (4 ounces) fresh green beans, cut into
    2-inch pieces
½ teaspoon garlic salt
¼ teaspoon dried rosemary, crushed
1 cup (1 large) thinly sliced zucchini
¾ cup (1 small) thinly sliced yellow squash
1½ cups (two 6-ounce jars) marinated
    artichoke hearts, undrained
1 cup frozen peas, thawed
½ teaspoon salt
¼ teaspoon ground black pepper
8 ounces dried fusilli pasta, cooked, drained
    and kept warm
¼ cup (1 ounce) grated Parmesan cheese

COMBINE tomatoes and juice, beans, garlic salt and rosemary in large skillet. Bring to a boil. Reduce heat to low; cook, covered, for 3 minutes.

ADD zucchini and squash; cover. Cook for 3 minutes or until vegetables are tender. Stir in artichoke hearts and marinade, peas, salt and pepper; heat through.

TOSS vegetables with pasta; sprinkle with cheese. *Makes 6 to 8 servings*

Italian Garden Fusilli

Cheese Ravioli with Wild Mushroom Sauce

2 tablespoons olive oil
1 medium onion, chopped
1 clove garlic, minced
8 ounces firm tofu, drained and cut into
    1-inch cubes
1½ cups ricotta cheese
1 cup grated Parmesan cheese, divided
½ teaspoon dried rosemary leaves
¼ teaspoon salt
64 plain or colored wonton wrappers
    (about 1⅓ packages)
    Wild Mushroom Sauce (recipe follows)

1. Heat oil in small skillet over medium heat.
Add onion and garlic; cook and stir 5 minutes or
until tender. Transfer to medium bowl. Process
tofu, ricotta cheese, ⅓ cup Parmesan, rosemary
and salt in food processor until smooth. Stir into
onion mixture.

2. To make ravioli, work with 8 wonton wrappers
at a time, keeping remaining wrappers covered
with plastic wrap. Place about 1 tablespoon
cheese mixture in center of each of 4 wonton
wrappers. Brush edges of wrappers with water.

3. Place second wrapper over filling and press
edges together to seal. Cover with plastic wrap
and set aside. Repeat with remaining wrappers
and cheese mixture. Prepare Wild Mushroom
Sauce; keep warm.

4. Bring water to a boil in Dutch oven or large
saucepan over high heat. Drop 8 ravioli into
boiling water; cook, uncovered, 3 to 4 minutes
or until ravioli float and are just tender. Remove

to warm platter with slotted spoon. Repeat with
remaining ravioli.

5. Place 4 ravioli on each serving plate; spoon
Wild Mushroom Sauce over ravioli and sprinkle
with remaining ⅔ cup Parmesan cheese.

Makes 8 servings

Wild Mushroom Sauce

3 tablespoons olive oil
12 ounces shiitake or porcini mushrooms,
    wiped, stemmed and sliced
6 ounces cremini or button mushrooms,
    wiped and sliced
1½ cups sliced green onions and tops
1 tablespoon dried basil leaves
½ to 1 teaspoon dried thyme leaves
3 cups vegetable broth, divided
1½ tablespoons cornstarch
2 tablespoons minced parsley
½ teaspoon salt
4 to 6 dashes hot pepper sauce

1. Heat oil in large skillet over medium heat until
hot. Add mushrooms, green onions, basil and
thyme; cook and stir 5 minutes or until
mushrooms release liquid. Continue cooking
10 minutes or until mushrooms have darkened
and all liquid is evaporated, stirring occasionally.

2. Add 2¾ cups broth; bring to a boil. Reduce
heat to medium-low and simmer, uncovered,
10 to 12 minutes or until broth is reduced by one-
third. Return liquid to a boil. Combine cornstarch
and remaining ¼ cup broth in small cup. Add to
mushroom mixture. Boil, stirring constantly, 1 to 2
minutes or until thickened. Stir in parsley, salt
and pepper sauce.   *Makes about 3 cups sauce*

Cheese Ravioli with Wild Mushroom Sauce

Penne with Creamy Tomato Sauce

1 tablespoon olive or vegetable oil
½ cup chopped onion
2 tablespoons dry vermouth or white wine
8 ounces dried penne pasta, cooked, drained, kept warm
1¾ cups (14.5-ounce can) CONTADINA® Dalla Casa Buitoni Pasta Ready Chunky Tomatoes with Olive Oil, Garlic & Spices, undrained
1 cup (3.8-ounce can) sliced ripe olives, drained
½ cup heavy whipping cream
½ cup (2 ounces) grated Parmesan cheese Sliced green onions

HEAT oil in large skillet over medium-high heat. Add onion; cook for 2 minutes. Add vermouth; cook for 1 minute. Add pasta, tomatoes and juice, olives, cream and cheese; toss well.

COOK for 2 to 3 minutes. Sprinkle with green onions. *Makes 4 servings*

Pasta & Vegetable Medley

1 cup uncooked macaroni
1 bag (16 ounces) BIRDS EYE® frozen Farm Fresh Mixtures Brussels Sprouts, Cauliflower & Carrots
2 tablespoons water
2 packages (3 ounces each) cream cheese, cubed
2 teaspoons chopped fresh basil or dill

• In large saucepan, cook macaroni according to package directions; drain in colander and rinse. Keep warm.

• Meanwhile, in large skillet, place vegetables and water; bring to boil over high heat. Reduce heat to medium; cover and simmer 6 to 8 minutes or until vegetables are crisp-tender.

• Remove skillet from heat; stir in cheese and basil. Add salt and pepper to taste.

• Stir in macaroni; cook until heated through. *Makes 4 servings*

Prep Time: 6 minutes
Cook Time: 20 minutes

Variations: For a hearty dish, add bacon bits, cubed cooked chicken, cooked seafood or ham. For a creamier dish, add a few tablespoons water; blend well and cook a little longer.

Penne with Creamy Tomato Sauce

Ravioli with Creamy Spinach Sauce

1 package (24 ounces) frozen beef ravioli
1 box (10 ounces) BIRDS EYE® frozen
   Chopped Spinach
1 jar (14.5 ounces) alfredo pasta sauce*
¼ teaspoon ground nutmeg
1 cup chopped tomato or roasted red pepper

*Or, substitute 1 packet (1.6 ounces) alfredo pasta sauce mix prepared according to package directions.

• In large saucepan, cook ravioli according to package directions; drain and set aside.

• Cook spinach according to package directions; place in strainer. Press excess water from spinach with back of spoon.

• In same saucepan, place spinach, alfredo sauce and nutmeg; cook over medium heat until heated through.

• Add ravioli and tomato; toss together.
Makes 4 servings

Prep Time: 5 minutes
Cook Time: 20 minutes

Chicken Pesto Mozzarella

6 to 8 ounces linguine or corkscrew pasta
4 half boneless chicken breasts, skinned
1 tablespoon olive oil
1 can (14½ ounces) DEL MONTE®
   FreshCut™ Diced Tomatoes with Basil,
   Garlic & Oregano, undrained
½ medium onion, chopped
⅓ cup sliced ripe olives
4 teaspoons pesto sauce*
¼ cup (1 ounce) shredded mozzarella cheese

*Pesto sauce is available frozen or refrigerated at the supermarket.

1. Cook pasta according to package directions; drain.

2. Meanwhile, season chicken with salt and pepper, if desired. In large skillet, brown chicken in hot oil over medium-high heat. Add tomatoes, onion and olives; bring to boil. Cover and cook 8 minutes over medium heat.

3. Remove cover; cook about 8 minutes or until chicken is no longer pink in center.

4. Spread 1 teaspoon pesto over each chicken breast; top with cheese. Cover and cook until cheese is melted. Serve over pasta. Garnish, if desired.
Makes 4 servings

Prep Time: 10 minutes
Cook Time: 25 minutes

Ravioli with Creamy Spinach

Thai Turkey & Noodles

1 package (about 1½ pounds) turkey
    tenderloins, cut into ¾-inch pieces
1 red bell pepper, cut into short, thin strips
1¼ cups reduced-sodium chicken broth,
    divided
¼ cup reduced-sodium soy sauce
3 cloves garlic, minced
¾ teaspoon crushed red pepper flakes
¼ teaspoon salt
2 tablespoons cornstarch
3 green onions, cut into ½-inch pieces
⅓ cup creamy or chunky peanut butter
    (not natural-style)
12 ounces hot cooked vermicelli pasta
¾ cup peanuts or cashews, chopped
¾ cup cilantro, chopped

Place turkey, bell pepper, 1 cup broth, soy sauce, garlic, red pepper flakes and salt in slow cooker. Cover and cook on low 3 hours.

Mix cornstarch with remaining ¼ cup broth in small bowl until smooth. Turn slow cooker to high. Stir in green onions, peanut butter and cornstarch mixture. Cover and cook 30 minutes or until sauce is thickened and turkey is no longer pink in center. Stir well. Serve over vermicelli. Sprinkle with peanuts and cilantro.

Makes 6 servings

Lite Pad Thai

8 ounces linguine
½ pound skinless boneless chicken breast
¾ cup no-salt-added tomato juice
3 tablespoons KIKKOMAN® Lite Soy Sauce
1 tablespoon vinegar
2 teaspoons sugar
¾ teaspoon cornstarch
3 tablespoons vegetable oil, divided
8 ounces fresh bean sprouts, rinsed and
    drained
½ cup sliced green onions with tops
2 cloves garlic, minced
½ pound cooked baby shrimp, rinsed and
    drained
1 tablespoon minced fresh cilantro
  Lime wedges

Cook linguine according to package directions, omitting salt; drain. Cut chicken into thin strips. Combine tomato juice, lite soy sauce, vinegar, sugar and cornstarch; set aside. Heat 1 tablespoon oil in hot wok or large skillet over high heat. Add chicken; stir-fry 1 minute. Remove from wok. Heat remaining 2 tablespoons oil in wok. Add bean sprouts, onions and garlic; stir-fry 1 minute. Stir in linguine; cook 2 minutes or until thoroughly heated. Add chicken, shrimp, cilantro and tomato juice mixture. Cook and stir until sauce boils and thickens. Serve with lime wedges. Garnish with additional cilantro, if desired.

Makes 4 servings

Plum Chicken

6 ounces fresh uncooked Chinese egg
noodles
¼ cup plum preserves or jam
3 tablespoons rice wine vinegar
3 tablespoons reduced-sodium soy sauce
1 tablespoon cornstarch
3 teaspoons vegetable oil, divided
1 small red onion, thinly sliced
2 cups fresh snow peas, diagonally sliced
into ½-inch pieces
12 ounces boneless skinless chicken breasts,
cut into thin strips
4 medium plums or apricots, pitted and
sliced

Cook noodles according to package directions,
omitting salt. Drain and keep warm. Stir together
plum preserves, vinegar, soy sauce and cornstarch
in small bowl; set aside. Heat 2 teaspoons oil in
large nonstick skillet or wok. Add onion and
cook 2 minutes or until slightly softened. Add
snow peas and cook 3 minutes. Remove mixture
to bowl.

Heat remaining 1 teaspoon oil in skillet. Add
chicken and cook over medium-high heat 2 to
3 minutes or until no longer pink. Push chicken
to one side of skillet. Stir plum sauce; add to
skillet. Cook and stir until thick and bubbly. Add
vegetables and plums; stir to coat evenly. Cook
3 minutes or until heated through. Toss with
noodles and serve immediately.

Makes 4 servings

Chicken Chow Mein

1 pound boneless skinless chicken breasts,
cut into 1-inch pieces
2 cloves garlic, minced
1 teaspoon vegetable oil, divided
2 tablespoons reduced-sodium soy sauce
2 tablespoons dry sherry
1 package (6 ounces) frozen snow peas,
thawed, cut in half
3 large green onions, cut diagonally into
1-inch pieces
4 ounces uncooked Chinese egg noodles or
vermicelli, cooked, drained and rinsed
1 teaspoon Oriental sesame oil

Toss chicken with garlic in small bowl. Heat
½ teaspoon vegetable oil in wok or large nonstick
skillet over medium heat. Add chicken mixture;
stir-fry 3 minutes or until chicken is no longer
pink. Transfer to medium bowl; toss with soy
sauce and sherry.

Heat remaining ½ teaspoon vegetable oil in wok.
Add snow peas; stir-fry 1 minute. Add onions;
stir-fry 30 seconds. Add chicken mixture; stir-fry
1 minute. Add noodles to wok; stir-fry 2 minutes
or until heated through. Stir in sesame oil.
Garnish, if desired.   *Makes 4 servings*

Plum Chicken

Chicken and Vegetables with Mustard Sauce

1 tablespoon sugar
2 teaspoons cornstarch
1½ teaspoons dry mustard
2 tablespoons reduced-sodium soy sauce
2 tablespoons water
2 tablespoons rice vinegar
1 pound boneless skinless chicken breasts
4 teaspoons vegetable oil, divided
2 cloves garlic, minced
1 small red bell pepper, cut into short thin strips
½ cup thinly sliced celery
1 small onion, cut into thin wedges
3 cups hot cooked Chinese egg noodles (3 ounces uncooked)

Combine sugar, cornstarch and mustard in small bowl. Blend soy sauce, water and vinegar into cornstarch mixture until smooth. Cut chicken into 1-inch pieces. Heat 2 teaspoons oil in wok or large nonstick skillet over medium heat. Add chicken and garlic; stir-fry 3 minutes or until chicken is no longer pink. Remove and reserve.

Add remaining 2 teaspoons oil to wok. Add bell pepper, celery and onion; stir-fry 3 minutes or until vegetables are crisp-tender. Stir soy sauce mixture; add to wok. Cook and stir 30 seconds or until sauce boils and thickens. Return chicken with any accumulated juices to wok; heat through. Serve over Chinese noodles.   *Makes 4 servings*

Chicken Normandy with Noodles

2 whole boneless chicken breasts (about 1 pound), halved
Salt and ground black pepper
4 tablespoons margarine or butter, divided
¼ teaspoon dried thyme leaves (optional)
1 medium onion, chopped
1 large tart red apple, unpeeled, cored and chopped
½ cup apple juice
2 tablespoons dry white wine (optional)
1½ cups water
½ cup milk
1 package LIPTON® Noodles & Sauce— Alfredo
2 tablespoons finely chopped fresh parsley

Lightly season chicken with salt and pepper.

In 12-inch skillet, melt 2 tablespoons margarine over medium-high heat and cook chicken with thyme until chicken is no longer pink. Remove chicken from skillet; keep warm.

In same skillet, add onion and apple and cook until tender. Stir in apple juice and wine; simmer, uncovered, 2 minutes or until liquid is reduced by half. Return chicken to skillet and simmer, covered, 5 minutes.

Meanwhile, in medium saucepan, bring water, milk and remaining 2 tablespoons margarine to a boil. Stir in Noodles & Sauce—Alfredo. Boil over medium heat, stirring occasionally, 8 minutes or until noodles are tender. Stir in parsley and pepper. To serve, arrange chicken over noodles.
Makes about 4 servings

Chicken and Vegetables with Mustard Sauce

Pasta with White Beans and Mushrooms

2 tablespoons vegetable oil
1 pound fresh white mushrooms, halved or quartered
1 cup chopped onions
1 cup diced carrots
1 teaspoon minced garlic
1 can (19 ounces) white kidney beans, rinsed and drained
1 can (13¾ ounces) ready-to-serve chicken broth
8 ounces smoked ham, diced
1 teaspoon Italian seasoning
4 cups (8 ounces) uncooked wagon wheel pasta
1 cup diced tomato
  Salt and pepper (optional)
  Grated Parmesan cheese (optional)
  Chopped fresh parsley (optional)

Heat oil in heavy saucepan until hot. Add mushrooms, onions, carrots and garlic; cook, stirring frequently, 6 to 8 minutes or until vegetables are tender. Add beans, chicken broth, ham and Italian seasoning; bring to a boil. Reduce heat and simmer, covered, about 20 minutes.

Meanwhile, cook pasta according to package directions; drain. Transfer to large serving bowl. Stir tomato into saucepan; cook about 2 minutes or until heated through. Season with salt and pepper to taste, if desired. Spoon over pasta. Sprinkle with grated Parmesan cheese and fresh parsley, if desired. *Makes 4 servings*

Favorite recipe from **Mushroom Council**

California Walnut Noodles

½ cup nonfat yogurt
½ cup orange juice
3 tablespoons balsamic or wine vinegar
2 tablespoons brown sugar
2 teaspoons sesame oil
1½ teaspoons grated fresh ginger *or* ½ teaspoon powdered ginger
½ teaspoon red pepper flakes (optional)
2 cloves garlic, minced
  Salt to taste (optional)
12 ounces uncooked spaghetti or linguini
2 cups cooked diced boneless skinless white meat chicken
1 red or green bell pepper, halved, seeded and thinly sliced
1 cucumber, halved, seeded and thinly sliced
2 teaspoons minced jalapeño pepper
2 tablespoons chopped cilantro (optional)
½ cup chopped green onions
⅔ cup chopped California walnuts

To make dressing, whisk yogurt, orange juice, vinegar, sugar, oil, ginger, pepper flakes, if desired, garlic and salt to taste, if desired. Set aside.
Makes about 1¼ cups dressing

Cook pasta in boiling salted water until al dente. Drain; rinse well and drain again. Toss with ¾ cup dressing. Combine chicken, bell pepper, cucumber, jalapeño pepper, cilantro, if desired, and green onions with remaining dressing. Mound pasta on large platter or shallow bowl and spoon chicken mixture down center. Top with walnuts.
Makes 4 servings

Favorite recipe from **Walnut Marketing Board**

Seafood Primavera

⅓ cup olive oil
1 medium onion, chopped
4 green onions with tops, chopped
3 cloves garlic, minced
3 carrots, cut into julienne strips
1 zucchini, cut into julienne strips
1 *each* small red and yellow bell pepper, cut into strips
3 ounces snow peas
⅓ cup sliced mushrooms
½ pound *each* peeled and deveined medium shrimp and scallops
⅔ cup clam juice
⅓ cup dry white wine
1 cup heavy cream
½ cup freshly grated Parmesan cheese
⅔ cup flaked crabmeat
2 tablespoons *each* lemon juice and chopped fresh parsley
¼ teaspoon *each* dried basil and oregano leaves
Freshly ground black pepper to taste
1 package (8 ounces) linguine, cooked and drained

Heat oil in large skillet over medium-high heat. Add onions and garlic; cook and stir until tender. Add remaining vegetables. Reduce heat to medium-low; cover. Simmer until tender, stirring occasionally. Remove vegetable mixture from skillet; set aside.

Add shrimp and scallops to skillet; cook and stir until shrimp turn pink and scallops are opaque. Remove from skillet, reserving liquid in skillet.

Add clam juice and wine to skillet; bring to a boil. Stir in cream and Parmesan. Reduce heat; simmer 3 minutes until thickened, stirring constantly.

Return vegetables and seafood to skillet. Heat thoroughly, stirring occasionally. Stir in all remaining ingredients *except* linguine. Pour over hot linguine in large bowl; toss gently to coat.
Makes 6 servings

Spicy Mesquite Chicken Fettuccine

8 ounces uncooked fettuccine
1 tablespoon chili powder
1 teaspoon ground cumin
1 teaspoon paprika
¼ teaspoon ground red pepper
2 teaspoons vegetable oil
1 pound mesquite marinated chicken breasts, cut into bite-sized pieces

1. Cook pasta according to package directions, omitting salt. Drain; set aside.

2. Combine chili powder, cumin, paprika and ground red pepper in small bowl; set aside.

3. Heat oil in large nonstick skillet over medium-high heat until hot. Add chili powder mixture; cook 30 seconds, stirring constantly. Add chicken; cook and stir 5 to 6 minutes or until no longer pink in center and lightly browned. Add pasta to skillet; stir. Cook 1 to 2 minutes or until heated through. Sprinkle with additional chili powder, if desired. Garnish, if desired. *Makes 4 servings*

Shrimp & Snow Peas with Fusilli

6 ounces uncooked fusilli
2 cloves garlic, finely chopped
¼ teaspoon crushed red pepper
12 ounces medium shrimp, peeled and
    deveined
2 cups snow peas
1 can (8 ounces) sliced water chestnuts,
    drained
⅓ cup sliced green onions
3 tablespoons lime juice
2 tablespoons chopped fresh cilantro
2 tablespoons olive oil
1 tablespoon reduced sodium soy sauce
1½ teaspoons Mexican seasoning
    Sliced radishes for garnish

1. Cook pasta according to package directions, omitting salt; drain. Set aside.

2. Spray large nonstick skillet with nonstick cooking spray; heat over medium heat until hot. Add garlic and red pepper; stir-fry 1 minute. Add shrimp; stir-fry 5 minutes or until shrimp are opaque. Remove shrimp from skillet.

3. Add snow peas and 2 tablespoons water to skillet; cook, covered, 1 minute. Uncover; cook and stir 2 minutes or until snow peas are crisp-tender. Remove snow peas from skillet.

4. Combine pasta, shrimp, snow peas, water chestnuts and onions in large bowl. Blend lime juice, cilantro, oil, soy sauce and Mexican seasoning in small bowl. Drizzle over pasta mixture; toss to coat. Garnish with radishes, if desired. *Makes 6 servings*

Broccoli and Cauliflower Linguine

2 tablespoons olive or vegetable oil
2 cups broccoli flowerets
2 cups cauliflowerets
3 cloves garlic, minced
3½ cups (28-ounce can) CONTADINA®
    Dalla Casa Buitoni Pasta Ready
    Chunky Tomatoes with Olive Oil,
    Garlic, Basil and Spices, undrained
1 teaspoon salt
¼ teaspoon crushed red pepper flakes
½ cup dry sherry or chicken broth
1 pound dry linguine, cooked, drained, kept
    warm
½ cup (2 ounces) grated Romano cheese
½ cup finely chopped fresh cilantro

HEAT oil in large skillet. Add broccoli, cauliflower and garlic; sauté for 3 minutes.

ADD tomatoes and juice, salt and red pepper flakes. Bring to a boil. Reduce heat to low; simmer, uncovered, for 20 minutes, stirring occasionally. Add sherry; simmer for 3 minutes.

PLACE pasta in large bowl. Add vegetable mixture, cheese and cilantro; toss to coat well.
Makes 8 servings

Shrimp & Snow Peas with Fusilli

Tortellini with Salmon & Dill

1 package (8 ounces) PHILADELPHIA
    BRAND® Cream Cheese, cubed
⅓ cup milk
½ cup chopped cucumber
3 ounces smoked salmon, cut into thin strips
2 teaspoons chopped fresh dill *or* ½ teaspoon
    dill weed
1 package (9 ounces) DI GIORNO® Cheese
    Tortellini, cooked, drained

STIR cream cheese and milk in medium saucepan on low heat until smooth. Add cucumber, salmon and dill; heat thoroughly.

TOSS with hot tortellini. Garnish, if desired.
Makes 4 servings

Prep Time: 20 minutes
Cook Time: 10 minutes

Lemon-Basil Pasta

8 ounces linguine or other pasta
2 tablespoons butter or margarine, melted
1 tablespoon lemon juice
1½ teaspoons McCORMICK® Basil Leaves
¾ teaspoon McCORMICK® Garlic Salt
¼ teaspoon McCORMICK® Ground Black
    Pepper
¼ cup grated Parmesan cheese

1. Cook pasta in unsalted water according to package directions. Drain pasta and return to pot.

2. Combine melted butter, lemon juice, basil, garlic salt, and pepper in small bowl. Add to cooked pasta and toss gently.

3. Spoon into serving dish and sprinkle with cheese. Garnish with lemon slices and fresh basil leaves, if desired. *Makes 4 servings*

White Tie and Tails

8 ounces Bow Ties, Radiatore or other
    medium pasta shape, uncooked
1 cup half-and-half
½ cup crumbled blue cheese
½ cup grated low-fat Swiss cheese
½ cup grated Romano cheese
¼ cup grated low-sodium Parmesan cheese
⅓ cup ¼-inch prosciutto strips
2 tablespoons chopped fresh basil *or*
    2 teaspoons dried basil

Cook pasta according to package directions. Meanwhile, heat half-and-half in 2-quart saucepan over medium heat; do not boil. Add blue, Swiss and Romano cheeses. Reduce heat; cook and stir until cheeses are blended and sauce is smooth; remove from heat.

When pasta is done, drain well. Pour sauce over cooked pasta; toss. Sprinkle with Parmesan cheese, prosciutto and basil. Serve immediately.
Makes 4 entrée servings

Favorite recipe from **National Pasta Association**

Tortellini with Salmon & Dill

Penne with Arrabiatta Sauce

½ pound uncooked penne or other
  tube-shaped pasta
2 tablespoons olive oil or oil from sun-dried
  tomatoes
8 cloves garlic
1 can (28 ounces) crushed tomatoes in
  purée
¼ cup chopped sun-dried tomatoes packed
  in oil
3 tablespoons FRANK'S® Original
  REDHOT® Cayenne Pepper Sauce
8 Kalamata olives, pitted and chopped*
6 fresh basil leaves or 1½ teaspoons dried
  basil leaves
1 tablespoon capers

*To pit olives, place olives on cutting board. Press with
side of knife until olives split. Remove pits.

1. Cook pasta according to package directions;
drain.

2. Heat oil in large nonstick skillet over medium
heat. Add garlic; cook until golden, stirring
frequently. Add remaining ingredients. Bring to
a boil. Simmer, partially covered, 10 minutes. Stir
occasionally.

3. Toss pasta with *half* of the sauce mixture.
Spoon into serving bowl. Pour remaining sauce
mixture over pasta. Garnish with fresh basil or
parsley, if desired.   *Makes 4 servings*
                              (3 cups sauce)

Prep Time: 15 minutes
Cook Time: 20 minutes

Pasta with Shrimp, Broccoli and Red Pepper

8 ounces uncooked capellini, linguine or
  thin spaghetti
2 tablespoons FILIPPO BERIO® Olive Oil
1 medium onion, finely chopped
1 clove garlic, minced
1 bunch fresh broccoli, trimmed and
  separated into florets
½ cup chicken broth
8 ounces cooked, peeled and deveined
  shrimp
1 red bell pepper, seeded and thinly sliced
2 tablespoons chopped fresh Italian parsley
1 fresh jalapeño pepper, seeded and minced
  Salt and freshly ground black pepper

Cook pasta according to package directions until
al dente (tender but still firm). Drain. In large
saucepan or Dutch oven, heat olive oil over
medium heat until hot. Add onion and garlic;
cook and stir 5 minutes or until onion is tender.
Add broccoli and chicken broth. Cover; reduce
heat to low and simmer 8 to 10 minutes or until
broccoli is tender-crisp. Add shrimp, bell pepper,
parsley and jalapeño pepper; stir occasionally
until heated through. Add pasta to broccoli
mixture; toss until lightly coated. Season to taste
with salt and black pepper.   *Makes 4 servings*

Penne with Arrabiatta Sauce

Skillet Shrimp with Rotelle

3 tablespoons FILIPPO BERIO® Olive Oil
1 medium onion, chopped
2 cloves garlic, minced
2 cups uncooked rotelle or other curly pasta
3 cups chicken broth
1 cup asparagus tips
¾ pound raw medium shrimp, shelled and deveined
¾ cup halved cherry tomatoes
¼ cup pitted ripe olives
1 teaspoon dried oregano leaves
1 teaspoon dried basil leaves
    Salt and freshly ground black pepper

In large skillet, heat olive oil over medium heat until hot. Add onion and garlic; cook and stir 4 to 6 minutes or until onion is softened but not brown.

Add pasta; stir to coat pasta with oil. Increase heat to high; pour in chicken broth. Bring to a boil. Reduce heat to medium-high; cook, stirring occasionally, 12 to 14 minutes or until pasta is al dente (*tender but still firm*). Add asparagus. Cook, stirring frequently, 2 to 3 minutes or until asparagus is tender-crisp.

Add shrimp, tomatoes, olives, oregano and basil. Cook, stirring frequently, 3 minutes or until liquid is almost completely absorbed and shrimp are opaque (*do not overcook shrimp*). Season to taste with salt and pepper.

Makes 4 to 6 servings

Pasta with Spinach-Cheese Sauce

¼ cup FILIPPO BERIO® Extra-Virgin Flavorful Olive Oil, divided
1 medium onion, chopped
1 clove garlic, chopped
3 cups chopped fresh spinach, washed and well drained
1 cup low-fat ricotta or cottage cheese
½ cup chopped fresh parsley
1 teaspoon dried basil leaves, crushed
1 teaspoon lemon juice
¼ teaspoon black pepper
¼ teaspoon ground nutmeg
¾ pound uncooked spaghetti

1. Heat 3 tablespoons olive oil in large skillet over medium heat. Add onion and garlic; cook and stir until onion is tender.

2. Add spinach to skillet; cook 3 to 5 minutes or until spinach wilts.

3. Place spinach mixture, cheese, parsley, basil, lemon juice, pepper and nutmeg in covered blender container. Blend until smooth. Leave in blender, covered, to keep sauce warm.

4. Cook pasta according to package directions until tender. *Do not overcook.* Drain pasta, reserving ¼ cup water. Toss pasta with remaining 1 tablespoon olive oil in large bowl.

5. Add reserved ¼ cup water to sauce in blender. Blend; serve sauce over pasta.

Makes 4 servings

Skillet Shrimp with Rotelle

Scallops with Vermicelli

1 pound bay scallops
2 tablespoons fresh lemon juice
2 tablespoons chopped fresh parsley
2 tablespoons olive oil
2 tablespoons butter, divided
1 medium onion, chopped
1 clove garlic, minced
1½ cups canned Italian tomatoes, undrained
      and chopped
2 tablespoons chopped fresh basil *or*
      ½ teaspoon dried basil leaves
¼ teaspoon dried oregano leaves
¼ teaspoon dried thyme leaves
2 tablespoons heavy cream
   Dash ground nutmeg
12 ounces uncooked vermicelli, cooked and
      drained

Rinse scallops. Combine scallops, lemon juice and parsley in glass bowl. Cover; marinate in refrigerator while preparing sauce.

Heat oil and 1 tablespoon butter in large skillet over medium-high heat. Add onion and garlic; cook and stir until onion is tender. Add tomatoes with juice, basil, oregano and thyme. Reduce heat to low. Cover; simmer 30 minutes, stirring occasionally.

Drain scallops; discard marinade. Heat remaining 1 tablespoon butter in separate large skillet over medium heat. Add scallops; cook and stir about 2 minutes or until scallops are opaque. Stir in cream, nutmeg and tomato sauce mixture.

Pour sauce over vermicelli in large serving bowl; toss gently to coat. Garnish as desired.

Makes 4 servings

Favorite recipe from **New Jersey Department of Agriculture**

Clam and Corn Linguine

1 package (8 ounces) linguine
1 jar (12 ounces) white clam sauce
1 box (10 ounces) BIRDS EYE® frozen
      Sweet Corn
1 cup water
1 chicken bouillon cube
½ cup chopped tomato
¼ cup grated Parmesan cheese

• In large saucepan, cook linguine according to package directions; drain.

• Meanwhile, in medium saucepan, bring clam sauce, corn, water and bouillon to boil over high heat. Reduce heat to medium and simmer 12 minutes or until heated through, stirring occasionally.

• In large bowl, toss linguine with sauce mixture. Sprinkle with tomato and cheese.

Makes 4 servings

Prep Time: 5 minutes
Cook Time: 12 to 15 minutes

Scallops with Vermicelli

Red Pepper & White Bean Pasta Sauce

12 ounces uncooked penne or ziti pasta
1 teaspoon olive oil
3 cloves garlic, chopped
1 jar (11.5 ounces) GUILTLESS
  GOURMET® Roasted Red Pepper Salsa
¾ cup canned cannellini beans (white kidney
  beans), rinsed well
½ cup low-sodium chicken or vegetable
  broth, defatted
⅓ cup chopped fresh cilantro
¼ cup crumbled feta cheese
  Fresh thyme sprigs (optional)

Cook pasta according to package directions. Drain and keep warm.

Meanwhile, heat oil in medium nonstick skillet over medium-high heat until hot. Add garlic; cook and stir 30 seconds or until softened. *Do not brown.* Add salsa, beans, broth and cilantro; bring just to a boil, stirring occasionally. (If mixture appears too thick, add water, 1 tablespoon at a time, to desired consistency.) To serve, place pasta in large serving bowl. Add salsa mixture; toss to coat well. Sprinkle with feta cheese. Garnish with thyme, if desired.   *Makes 4 servings*

Spaghetti with Roasted Zucchini and Olives

1 pound Spaghetti, Thin Spaghetti or
  Linguine, uncooked
3 medium zucchini, sliced into ½-inch slices
1 teaspoon vegetable oil
2 medium onions, chopped
3 cloves garlic, minced
1 (12-ounce) jar roasted peppers, drained
  (liquid reserved) and diced
12 black olives, sliced
½ teaspoon crushed red pepper flakes
  Salt and pepper to taste
¼ cup crumbled feta cheese

Prepare pasta according to package directions. Drain and rinse with cold water; drain again.

Preheat oven to 500°F. Spray 2 large cookie sheets with vegetable oil cooking spray. Place zucchini on prepared sheets and coat with cooking spray. Roast zucchini in oven 8 to 10 minutes or until tender. Transfer to large bowl.

Heat vegetable oil in medium nonstick skillet over medium heat. Add onion and garlic; sauté 5 minutes or until lightly browned.

Add onion mixture, roasted peppers, olives, red pepper flakes and pasta to zucchini. Toss well. Season with salt and pepper. Sprinkle with feta cheese.   *Makes 4 servings*

Favorite recipe from **National Pasta Association**

Red Pepper & White Bean Pasta Sauce

Sweet & Sour Mustard Pork

1 pound boneless pork, cut into strips
¼ cup GREY POUPON® Dijon Mustard, divided
3 teaspoons soy sauce, divided
1 (3-ounce) package chicken-flavored Ramen noodles
1 (8-ounce) can pineapple chunks, drained, reserving juice
½ cup water
2 tablespoons packed light brown sugar
½ teaspoon grated fresh ginger
1 tablespoon cornstarch
2 cups broccoli flowerettes
½ cup chopped red or green cabbage
½ cup chopped red bell pepper
½ cup coarsely chopped onion
2 tablespoons vegetable oil

In medium bowl, combine pork strips, 2 tablespoons mustard and 1 teaspoon soy sauce. Refrigerate for 1 hour.

In small bowl, combine remaining mustard and soy sauce, chicken flavor packet from noodles, reserved pineapple juice, water, brown sugar, ginger and cornstarch; set aside. Cook Ramen noodles according to package directions; drain and set aside.

In large skillet, over medium-high heat, stir-fry vegetables in oil until tender-crisp; remove from skillet. Add pork mixture; stir-fry for 3 to 4 minutes or until done. Return vegetables to skillet with pineapple chunks and cornstarch mixture; heat until mixture thickens and begins to boil. Add cooked noodles, tossing to coat well.

Makes 4 servings

Pasta Stew with Rosemary Pork

8 ounces Ditalini, Orzo or Alphabets, uncooked
1 teaspoon vegetable oil
1 pound lean, boneless pork loin, cut into ¾-inch cubes
⅛ teaspoon ground red pepper
⅛ teaspoon black pepper
3 (13¼ ounce) cans fat-free, low-sodium beef broth, divided
1 cup chopped onion
½ cup chopped celery
1½ tablespoons minced fresh rosemary *or* 1½ teaspoons dried rosemary
½ teaspoon salt
2 medium sweet potatoes, peeled and cut into 1-inch cubes (about 3 cups)
2 cups chopped fresh spinach
2 tablespoons lime juice

Heat oil in large saucepan or Dutch oven until heated. Add pork; cook about 4 to 5 minutes or until no longer pink. Drain well. Toss pork with red and black pepper in medium bowl; set aside.

Add ¼ cup beef broth, onion and celery to saucepan. Cook and stir until onion is tender. Add pork, remaining beef broth, rosemary and salt. Bring to a boil. Add pasta and sweet potatoes and boil, stirring occasionally, 10 to 15 minutes or until pasta is done. Stir in spinach and lime juice. (Stew will continue to absorb liquid.) Serve immediately.   *Makes 6 servings*

Favorite recipe from **National Pasta Association**

Sweet & Sour Mustard Pork

Tri-Color Pasta

1 package (16 ounces) tri-color pasta*
2 cups BIRDS EYE® frozen Green Peas
2 plum tomatoes, chopped *or* 1 red bell
    pepper, chopped
1 cup shredded mozzarella cheese
⅓ cup prepared pesto sauce, or to taste

*Or, substitute 1 bag (16 ounces) frozen tortellini.

• In large saucepan, cook pasta according to package directions. Add peas during last 5 minutes; drain in colander. Rinse under cold water to cool.

• In large bowl, combine pasta, peas, tomatoes and cheese. Stir in pesto.　*Makes 4 servings*

Prep Time: 5 minutes

Cook Time: 10 minutes

Rigatoni with Broccoli

8 ounces uncooked rigatoni pasta
1 bunch fresh broccoli, trimmed and
    separated into florets with 1-inch stems
1 tablespoon FILIPPO BERIO® Extra Virgin
    Olive Oil
1 clove garlic, minced
    Crushed red pepper
    Grated Parmesan cheese

Cook pasta according to package directions until al dente (tender but still firm). Add broccoli during last 5 minutes of cooking time; cook until broccoli is tender-crisp. Drain pasta and broccoli; transfer to large bowl. Meanwhile, in small skillet, heat olive oil over medium heat until hot. Add garlic; cook and stir 1 to 2 minutes or until golden. Pour oil mixture over hot pasta mixture; toss until lightly coated. Season to taste with pepper. Top with cheese.　*Makes 3 to 4 serving*

Bow Ties with Vegetables Alfredo

1 package (8 ounces) bow tie pasta
1 bag (16 ounces) BIRDS EYE® frozen
    Farm Fresh Mixtures Broccoli,
    Cauliflower & Carrots
1 packet (1.6 ounces) alfredo pasta
    sauce mix
1 cup whole milk
½ cup water
1 teaspoon butter
½ teaspoon pepper

• In large saucepan, cook pasta according to package directions. Add vegetables during last 5 minutes; drain and return to saucepan.

• Meanwhile, in medium saucepan, prepare sauce according to package directions using milk, water and butter.

• Stir sauce into vegetables and pasta; cook over medium heat until heated through.

• Season with pepper.　*Makes 4 servings*

Prep Time: 5 minutes

Cook Time: 20 minutes

Variation: Stir in prepared pesto sauce to taste with alfredo sauce.

Tri-Color Pasta

Stuffed Jumbo Shells with Garlic Vegetables

Garlic Vegetables (recipe follows)
12 jumbo pasta shells
 1 package (10 ounces) frozen chopped
    spinach, thawed
 2 cups ricotta cheese
¼ cup grated Parmesan cheese
 2 cloves garlic, minced
¾ teaspoon dried marjoram leaves
½ teaspoon dried basil leaves
¼ teaspoon dried thyme leaves
½ to 1 teaspoon salt
½ teaspoon black pepper
   Freshly grated Parmesan cheese

1. Prepare Garlic Vegetables. Spoon into bottom of 10-inch round baking dish.

2. Cook shells according to package directions. Drain; cool.

3. Using back of wooden spoon, press spinach to remove excess moisture.

4. Combine ricotta, spinach, ¼ cup Parmesan, garlic, marjoram, basil, thyme, salt and pepper in medium bowl. Spoon cheese mixture into shells.

5. Preheat oven to 350°F. Arrange shells on top of Garlic Vegetables. Carefully spoon sauce from vegetables over shells.

6. Bake, loosely covered with foil, 35 to 40 minutes or until stuffed shells are heated through. Serve with freshly grated Parmesan cheese.

Makes 4 servings

Garlic Vegetables

 2 tablespoons olive oil, divided
 1 large head garlic, peeled and coarsely
    chopped
⅓ cup sun-dried tomatoes (not packed in oil)
 2 tablespoons all-purpose flour
1¼ cups canned vegetable broth
 2 large carrots, peeled and cut into ¼-inch
    slices
 1 medium zucchini, cut lengthwise in half
    and sliced
 1 medium yellow summer squash, cut
    lengthwise in half and sliced
 2 tablespoons minced fresh parsley
   Salt
   Black pepper

1. Heat 1 tablespoon oil in small skillet over medium heat until hot. Add garlic; cook and stir 2 to 3 minutes. Reduce heat to low and cook about 15 minutes or until garlic is golden brown, stirring frequently.

2. Add tomatoes; cook over medium heat 2 minutes. Stir in flour. Cook and stir 2 minutes. Gradually stir in broth. Cook 1 to 2 minutes or until sauce thickens, stirring constantly.

3. Heat remaining 1 tablespoon oil in medium skillet over medium heat until hot. Add carrots; cook and stir 2 minutes. Add zucchini and squash; cook and stir 3 minutes or until crisp-tender. Remove from heat.

4. Stir garlic mixture and parsley into carrot mixture in skillet. Season to taste with salt and pepper.

Makes 2 cups

Stuffed Jumbo Shells with Garlic Vegetables

Pasta with Onions and Goat Cheese

2 teaspoons olive oil
4 cups thinly sliced sweet onions
¾ cup (3 ounces) goat cheese
¼ cup skim milk
6 ounces uncooked baby bow tie or other small pasta
1 clove garlic, minced
2 tablespoons dry white wine or fat-free reduced-sodium chicken broth
1½ teaspoons chopped fresh sage *or* ½ teaspoon dried sage leaves
½ teaspoon salt
¼ teaspoon pepper
2 tablespoons chopped toasted walnuts

Heat oil in large nonstick skillet over medium heat. Add onions; cook slowly until golden and caramelized, about 20 to 25 minutes, stirring occasionally.

Combine goat cheese and milk in small bowl; stir until well blended. Set aside.

Cook pasta according to package directions, omitting salt. Drain and set aside.

Add garlic to onions in skillet; cook until softened, about 3 minutes. Add wine, sage, salt and pepper; cook until moisture is evaporated. Remove from heat; add pasta and goat cheese mixture, stirring to melt cheese. Sprinkle with walnuts. *Makes 8 (½-cup) servings*

Mediterranean Pasta

6 to 8 ounces vermicelli
2 half boneless chicken breasts, skinned and cut into 1½×½-inch strips
4 slices bacon, diced
1 can (14½ ounces) DEL MONTE® *FreshCut*™ Diced Tomatoes with Garlic & Onion
1 can (15 ounces) DEL MONTE® Tomato Sauce
½ teaspoon dried rosemary, crushed
1 package (9 ounces) frozen artichoke hearts, thawed
½ cup pitted ripe olives, sliced lengthwise

1. Cook pasta according to package directions; drain.

2. Meanwhile, season chicken with salt and pepper, if desired. In large skillet, cook bacon over medium-high heat until almost crisp. Add chicken; cook until browned on both sides. Drain.

3. Stir in tomatoes, tomato sauce and rosemary. Cook 15 minutes, stirring occasionally. Add artichokes and olives; heat through.

4. Just before serving, spoon sauce over hot pasta. Garnish with crumbled feta cheese and chopped parsley, if desired. *Makes 4 to 6 servings*

Prep Time: 5 minutes

Cook Time: 30 minutes

Helpful Hint: Cook pasta ahead; rinse and drain. Cover and refrigerate. Just before serving, heat in microwave or dip into boiling water.

Pasta with Onions and Goat Cheese

Rigatoni with Four Cheeses

3 cups milk
1 tablespoon chopped carrot
1 tablespoon chopped celery
1 tablespoon chopped onion
1 tablespoon parsley sprigs
½ bay leaf
¼ teaspoon black peppercorns
¼ teaspoon hot pepper sauce
  Dash ground nutmeg
¼ cup butter
¼ cup all-purpose flour
½ cup grated Wisconsin Parmesan cheese
¼ cup grated Wisconsin Romano cheese
12 ounces uncooked rigatoni, cooked and
  drained
1½ cups (6 ounces) shredded Wisconsin
  Cheddar cheese
1½ cups (6 ounces) shredded Wisconsin
  mozzarella cheese
¼ teaspoon chili powder

Combine milk, carrot, celery, onion, parsley, bay
leaf, peppercorns, hot pepper sauce and nutmeg
in large saucepan. Bring to a boil. Reduce heat
to low; simmer 10 minutes. Strain; reserve liquid.

Preheat oven to 350°F. Melt butter in medium
saucepan over medium heat. Stir in flour.
Gradually stir in reserved liquid. Cook, stirring
constantly, until thickened. Remove from heat.
Add Parmesan and Romano cheeses; stir until
blended. Pour into large bowl. Add rigatoni; toss
gently to coat. Combine Cheddar and mozzarella
cheeses in medium bowl. Place half the rotini

mixture in greased 2-quart casserole; sprinkle
with cheese mixture. Top with remaining rotini
mixture. Sprinkle with chili powder. Bake
25 minutes or until bubbly. Garnish as desired.

Makes 6 servings

Favorite recipe from **Wisconsin Milk Marketing Board**

Pasta with Roasted Red Pepper Sauce

12 ounces uncooked linguine or spaghetti
1 can (28 ounces) low-sodium peeled,
  chopped tomatoes
1 jar (11.5 ounces) GUILTLESS
  GOURMET® Roasted Red Pepper Salsa
⅓ cup (about 18) crushed GUILTLESS
  GOURMET® Baked Tortilla Chips
  (yellow or white corn)
¼ cup chopped fresh cilantro

Cook pasta according to package directions.
Drain and keep warm.

Meanwhile, combine tomatoes and salsa in small
saucepan or microwave-safe dish; cook over
medium heat or microwave on HIGH (100%
power) until thoroughly heated. Place pasta on
serving platter; pour sauce over pasta. Sprinkle
with crushed chips and cilantro. Serve hot.

Makes 4 servings

Rigatoni with Four Cheeses

Oriental Beef & Noodle Toss

1 pound lean ground beef
2 packages (3 ounces each) Oriental flavor
    instant ramen noodles
2 cups water
2 cups frozen Oriental vegetable mixture
1/8 teaspoon ground ginger
2 tablespoons thinly sliced green onion

1. In large nonstick skillet, brown ground beef over medium heat 8 to 10 minutes, breaking up beef into 3/4-inch crumbles. Remove with slotted spoon; pour off drippings. Season beef with 1 seasoning packet from noodles; set aside.

2. In same skillet, combine water, frozen vegetables, noodles (broken into several pieces), ginger and remaining seasoning packet. Bring to a boil; reduce heat. Cover; simmer 3 minutes or until noodles are tender, stirring occasionally.

3. Return beef to skillet; heat through. Stir in green onion before serving.   *Makes 4 servings*

Favorite recipe from **National Cattlemen's Beef Association**

Stir-Fried Pork Lo Mein

6 green onions, cut into 1-inch pieces
1/2 teaspoon garlic powder
1/2 teaspoon ground ginger
6 ounces pork loin roast, thinly sliced
3 cups shredded green cabbage
1/2 cup shredded carrots
1/2 cup trimmed snow peas
1/2 cup 1/3-less-salt chicken broth
2 teaspoons cornstarch
2 tablespoons hoisin sauce (optional)
1 tablespoon reduced sodium soy sauce
8 ounces hot cooked linguine

1. Spray wok with nonstick cooking spray. Heat over medium heat until hot. Add onions, garlic powder and ginger; stir-fry 30 seconds. Add pork; stir-fry 2 minutes or until pork is no longer pink. Add vegetables; stir-fry 3 minutes or until vegetables are crisp-tender.

2. Blend chicken broth, cornstarch, hoisin sauce, if desired, and soy sauce in small bowl. Add to wok. Cook and stir until mixture boils and thickens. Serve vegetables and sauce over pasta.
Makes 4 servings